1/88 $8.^{50}$

BEGINNING KARATE

BEGINNING KARATE

David Mitchell

Published in association with
The Martial Arts Commission of
Great Britain

London
UNWIN PAPERBACKS
Boston   Sydney

First published in Great Britain by
Unwin Paperbacks 1987
Designed by Bob Vickers
Produced by The Bowerdean Press
London SW11
© Copyright The Bowerdean Press

UNWIN PAPERBACKS
Denmark House, 37-39 Queen Elizabeth Street
London SE1 2QB
and
40 Museum Street, London WC1A 1LU

Allen & Unwin Australia Pty Ltd
8 Napier Street, North Sydney, NSW 2060, Australia

Unwin Paperbacks with Port Nicholson Press
P O Box 11-838 Wellington, New Zealand

British Library Cataloguing in Publication Data
Mitchell, David, *1944-*
    Beginning Karate.
    1. Karate
    I. Title
    796.8'153   GV1114.3

    ISBN 0 04 440000 4

The Martial Arts are potentially
dangerous: the author, producers and
publishers will accept no liability for
damage or injuries resulting from the
performance of techniques described in
this book.

Typeset by TJB Photosetting Ltd.,
South Witham, Lincolnshire.

Printed and bound in England by R.J. Acford Ltd
Sussex

Contents

Kata training builds stamina, speed and strength. Constant repetition makes for fast reflexes.

Introduction

When I came across karate during Spring 1964, I wasn't sure exactly what it was. I gathered it was different from judo which suited me because I'd done a bit of that in the British Judo Association and found it not to my liking. Beyond that I knew very little except that it included some pretty powerful strikes, the most celebrated being the dreaded 'karate chop'.

My first proper teachers were Japanese and their methods of instruction were very traditional indeed! For example, the chap practising next to me during our second lesson, couldn't get his toes back for the front kick so the instructor timed his move exactly right and slid his knee forward into the path of the developing kick. This resulted in my fellow student fracturing his toes.

My turn was next. I was concentrating so singlemindedly on pulling my toes back that I left my groin open. "Crose gloin!" was the terse admonition I got by way of a warning. I straight-away fixed my attention on closing my thighs as I kicked and by default, let my toes curl down. This was not missed and I got a second warning – "Purr back toes!" So next time I concentrated on my toes.

My inability to concentrate on more than one thing at a time meant I'd (you've guessed it!) left my groin open and whilst I may have forgotten it, the instructor didn't. His foot lashed out, catching me sharply where it hurts most. For this I'd given up my weekend and paid a small fortune?

It wasn't the only time by a long chalk that I experienced that kind of instruction. Actually I must have been very favoured indeed because it was unusual to give one, let alone two warnings before using a more direct method of drawing attention to a fault. Part of the problem was that the Japanese spoke almost no English. Their verbal coaching ability was limited to the ones previously mentioned plus 'More quickwee', or 'More hiptwist'. If what they wanted to say fell outside of those narrow limits, they set to work kicking and thumping the offending part until the error was corrected.

Before you think me an arrant racist, I would point out that my next instructor was British (albeit Japanese trained!). His idea of a good training session was to drive us to the point of exhaustion and then bash us into insensibility for our pains! I well remember his week-long training course at Dale Fort in Pembrokeshire where we started off with 160 hopefuls and finished with 27!

If this is karate, why on God's earth would any sane person pay to put up with it? Can you imagine wanting to take up horse-riding and getting beaten up every time you got out of synch on the rising trot?

Yet that is what I and many others like me tolerated. Were we mad? No more so, I dare say, than the mountaineer who puts up with extreme hardship to climb a hazardous ice wall.

We were students of what was described as an oriental martial art and that made it all somehow different. Our teachers were not interested (at first, anyway) in teaching enormous classes of people who thought of karate as just another hobby to practise alongside birdwatching or rugby. They purposefully set out to winnow the numbers down by dint of applied sadism, until they were left with a small group of enthusiasts (lunatics?) who were prepared to take whatever was handed out.

I learned later in my martial arts career that this process is authentically Japanese and it is called *shugyo*, or 'austere training'. Its stated purpose is to concentrate the mind towards attaining a state of inner stillness which is vital to the attaining of true knowledge. By 'knowledge', I don't mean understanding exactly why I had to lift my hand this way and not that way, but a state of mind that I'm going to try and describe in a later chapter.

Somewhere along the line, less enlightened souls began to calculate that 50 less committed students at 50p brought in a lot more money than 10 keen ones and so the concept of 'leisure karate' evolved, leading to the establishment of quite large associations of clubs.

I don't know whether this was a good or a bad thing. On the one hand it popularised karate and made it into one of the world's fastest growing activities. On the other hand, it diluted karate.

I took up karate because I suppose I felt physically inadequate and wanted to be able to kick sand in people's eyes with impunity. That was the goal I started with. I soon came to realise that karate can't really help you achieve that aim. A coward who takes up karate merely becomes a cowardly *karateka* – one who practises karate – (and often concurrently a bully in the training hall).

Start by asking yourself why you want to train. Do you think that practising twice a week in your local church hall or local authority leisure centre will equip you to walk on rice paper without tearing it? Do you imagine that because you've got some practice time under your belt your hands and feet ought to be licensed as deadly weapons?

In this book I am going to try and do two things. Firstly I am going to make sure you know a sight more about karate than I did when I started. Secondly I hope to make you analyse what exactly you are doing in the hope that you will achieve a true understanding in the shortest possible time without the kind of apprenticeship I went through.

I have heard it said that since karate is an expression of Japanese culture, you can only truly understand it if you are Japanese yourself. My limited experience gained over a mere two decades is that this is not so. I have met people of many different nationalities who in my opinion truly understand karate. These are not specially gifted people, just students who have made karate their lifetime study and passed beyond the 'monkey see – monkey do' stage.

Mastering karate technique is simply a matter of physical training. Mastering karate requires far more; and the people I am speaking of have, in practical terms, achieved this. To be sure, they may have taken a different route to that set down in so called 'traditional' karate dogma but the end result is the same.

David Mitchell,
Penrith, 1986.

Kata training also promotes agility, speed and balance. Some moves are very graceful.

WHAT KARATE IS

Karate means three things to me. It is a fighting system, a combat sport and a system of mental/spiritual training.

Karate is sometimes called a 'martial art' but I don't know whether this is an accurate usage of the term. To me, a martial art should form part of a syllabus of military techniques used by the soldier on the battlefield. Karate was taught in schools as a means of generating a martial spirit and discipline but I'm not sure whether this qualifies it to be called a martial art.

Karate did not originate as a military art, you see. It was actually developed by peasants to allow them to defend themselves against robbers. To this end, a number of unorthodox weapons were employed and I will describe these later on. Weapon practice is now all but extinct in modern karate training halls.

Karate was a rural system of self defence. Although a pair of sickles don't look out of place in a farmer's field, they are conspicuous when carried about in the city. Some schools of karate therefore played down the weapon-using side and concentrated instead on empty hand techniques (from which, incidentally, karate derives its name).

It has been suggested that karate's peasant originators trained their hands and feet so they could punch or kick with enough force to injure an armoured Japanese warrior. My own opinion is that this is an exaggeration. Even allowing for the comparatively poor quality of latter-day Japanese conscripts, it still seems unlikely to me that any unarmed man can be seriously trained in the expectation of overcoming a weapon-bearing soldier. I once saw a good senior karateka lose repeatedly to a similarly qualified and uncooperative kendoka armed with a bamboo practice sword.

Whilst on the subject of comparisons, if I had a penny for every time I was asked which is the 'best' form of martial art, or the 'best' style of karate, I would be a rich man. It is the person practising the system, not the system itself which counts! To be sure, some systems have a smaller syllabus and are more quickly learned whilst others contain hundreds of techniques and take longer. Personally I don't like large syllabuses because when sparring, my mind can't choose quickly enough between the

options available. I would like to see a style of karate which con-
sisted of just one technique suitable for dealing with all situations!

Karate may not be a martial art per se but it is certainly a
system of fighting, or 'fighting art' if you prefer. It could also be
classified under the name of 'unarmed combat' since it uses
nothing but the body's natural weapons. The way in which these
weapons are used is quite different to say, judo. In the latter system, the body is used as a system of leverage to unbalance, throw
and hold the opponent. In karate, the arms and legs are used in
a striking mode and throws and locks are rarely taught.

The blows can develop a lot of force, as you will soon come to
find out and if they are applied to a vulnerable part of your opponent's anatomy, the result can be quite surprising. I don't think
that karateka produce harder punches than, say boxers but
karate does teach you how to generate the maximum power from
your strikes in a scientific and understandable way.

You may have seen karateka breaking bricks and thick boards
and if this sort of thing appeals to you, then you can learn how
to do it. It is a technique and needs much training to master.
Personally I treasure the delicate joints of my hands and regret
the damage I did to them during my earlier training days. There
are much better ways of testing how much power you can generate!

Karate is also a combat sport. In this respect it is like judo.
Both started off as pure fighting systems and through a process
of evolution (or, as some traditionalists would say, devolution),
the less controllable and nastier elements were discarded and a
set of rules introduced.

Karate the combat sport is great fun and enjoyed by people of
all ages. Unfortunately it does suffer badly from its rules and my
favourite description of it comes from an article I read in a
Sunday paper which described it as 'punch-up interruptus'.
This is because every time someone scores, the referee has to
stop the bout and agree with the judge on its merits. I love the
description of the referee's function as defined by the Chief
Referee of the World Union of Karate Organisations, George
Anderson. He says, and I quote 'The job of the referee is to stop
the bout every time it starts to get interesting!'.

Because of this, plus the fact there are four people all milling
around in a small competition square, a lot of odd arm waving
by the officials and a deal of Japanese bafflegab, karate competition is not seen on the telly. This may well change in the future

but karate the combat sport will have to take a long and hard look at its rules first.

Karate is also a form of mental and spiritual training. You may notice I haven't described it as a method of physical training. That is intentional. To get the best benefit from your karate lesson you have to be fit. If you are heaving and straining just to keep up with the pace of training, then you surely won't be able to concentrate on the finer points of your technique. It is for this reason that I recommend taking a course of supplementary fitness exercises. Karate will no doubt improve various aspects of your fitness but that is incidental to the training.

I have always found formal meditation difficult though I firmly believe that it is one of the keys to effective karate. I am usually too hyperactive to sit still in the hope that my mind will become still. Funnily enough though, karate does provide a sort of dynamic meditation and as you concentrate on what you are doing, the other worries of the day seem to subside. I found this very useful when I was studying for my exams. When I got to the stage of reading to the bottom of a page without being able to remember what was printed on it, I would collect my karate suit and go off for a couple of hours training. This calmed and emptied my mind, so that additional storage space could be found.

Karate is not alone in doing this. Any form of training that concentrates your attention achieves the same effect. When you are fit enough and have assimilated the techniques you have been learning a smaller part of your mind keeps an eye on things while the rest is freed. If you train hard enough, the unallocated capacity remains unfocussed. When your actions are instinctive, your responses are quicker and more effective. This is the key to karate.

There are many other claims made for the mental benefits of karate, some of which involve an energy form called *ki*. I admit to being sceptical about this. On the one hand I realise the all-too-apparent shortcomings of modern science but this does not mean I believe in fairies at the bottom of the garden either! I have seen demonstrations of so called *ki* and I have seen similar results obtained from physical means. So reserve your judgement if you come into contact with claims that karate confers miraculous powers upon its serious students.

Karate as we mainly practise it today is based upon a Buddhist philosophy. Statements like *mizu no-kokoro* ('having a mind like water') are not uncommon in traditional texts and illustrate the strong spiritual foundations upon which the Japanese created the form of karate known as *karate-do*, the 'way' of karate.

This sort of development is common in the Japanese fighting systems. For example, swordfighting was the warrior's mainstay and a manual of effective techniques was assembled through the natural selection of continuous warfare. These techniques were known as *ken jutsu*. When the sword was superseded by the gun, sword practice was retained but for a different purpose. It was no longer important to practise to be able to kill an adversary but more important to cultivate a martial spirit. 'Sword techniques' became 'the way of the sword', or kendo.

Previously karate was of the *jutsu* type, its techniques designed purely for effectiveness in combat. With the introduction of the *do* variety, many techniques and applications were de-emphasized and the method of teaching changed to suit larger classes. This principally involved serialisation of technique practice, with individual moves performed to a count. When taught to smaller classes as a fighting system, the teaching method was modular with several techniques taught in an uninterrupted unit. I personally prefer this latter method because when techniques are learned in isolation, it is difficult to link them afterwards.

Unfortunately in the competition to attract new members, a brand image is important and once the new *do* format became established, others had to follow suit. I personally regret this change and feel that karate has lost by it.

THE HISTORY OF KARATE

Karate as we practise it today is relatively modern. Like most fighting systems it is based upon much older forms of combat, principally those derived from the long hand Southern Shaolin boxing schools of mainland China. These are 'hard' systems, meaning that muscular effort plays a large part in the development of their powerful punches and kicks. They also utilise solid stances and long-range techniques. Classic karate shares these characteristics though in some later Japanese-developed styles, small changes have been introduced. In general terms though, karate remains a mid- to long range fighting system using strong stances and techniques which travel over a fair distance.

The immediate ancestor of modern karate is *to-te*, sometimes called *okinawa te*. It was developed on the island of Okinawa, the latter being the largest of the Ryukyu chain of islands which form a natural bridge between Japan and China. This geographical position and Okinawa's foreign policies led to the presence on the island of a Chinese delegation which included soldiers and military attaches. These were conspicuous for their contributions to Okinawan martial art training.

These contributions were incorporated into various schools and some Okinawan students visited the mainland to further their martial art studies. These brought back new ideas to throw into the melting pot that eventually became known either as *karate* ('China hand'), or *Ryukyu kempo* ('Ryukyu boxing').

Just as there were many schools of Chinese martial art, there were many Okinawan parallels. For convenience sake these were categorised according to whether they were the principal form practised in Naha, Tomari, or Shuri – the latter being the capital. The principal characteristic of the Naha forms was that of circular movements and solid stances. The Shuri schools tended to favour more direct and also faster movements. The Tomari schools exhibited the characteristics of both.

These schools practised secretly, not wishing any undeserving outsider to learn their specialised techniques. Owing to the bad relations which existed between the Japanese overlords and the Okinawan natives, the techniques of karate were kept hidden. The Japanese were not unaware of its existence though because the fighting system figured prominently in some of the local insurrections which flared up when the Japanese attempted to apply sanctions of one form or another.

Towards the end of the 19th century, this mutual antipathy abated and the Okinawans were prevailed upon by the Japanese navy to give a demonstration of karate. The Okinawans selected a schoolteacher by the name of Gichin Funakoshi to give the demonstration. Funakoshi was a good ambassador by virtue of his learning. This was important because the Japanese tended to regard the Okinawans as country bumpkins. He was also the student of the respected masters Itosu and Azato and so had good training credentials.

Funakoshi's demonstration was well received and he was invited to give a further one on the strength of it. Eventually he decided to resign from teaching and began to teach karate in Tokyo. Whilst there, he met the founder of Judo, Jigoro Kano. Both men were impressed with each other's practice and Funakoshi decided to alter the format of karate with the object of making it easier to teach and more acceptable to the Japanese.

The first change he made was in the name. By means of a change in the Japanese character, the meaning but not the pronounciation was changed from *karate* meaning 'China hand', to *karate do* meaning 'the way of the empty hand'. Other changes followed and the karate school founded by Funakoshi became known as *shotokan*. This is a play on Funakoshi's pen-name – *Shoto* meaning 'waving pines'.

Funakoshi was by no means the only Okinawan to have an effect upon Japanese karate but it is fair to attribute to him the major influence during those early days. Another Okinawan master was Chojun Miyagi, a follower of the Naha schools. The influence of Chinese martial arts on karate was still strong and Miyagi travelled to the mainland to learn more advanced forms. He evidently encountered some of the 'soft' schools there because he became aware of ways to develop power other than through the application of brute force. The incorporation of this within his style produced a curious blending which is recognised in the name of his school – *goju-ryu* – meaning 'hard/soft school'.

Kenwa Mabuni, an Okinawan policeman, was a contemporary of Miyagi. He obtained a vast knowledge of karate by studying under masters of all three Okinawan karate categories. The style which he founded has the largest syllabus of katas of any in karate. It is called *shito ryu*, this deriving from the names of his teachers.

The other major school is that founded by the senior Japanese student of Funakoshi – Hironori Ohtsuka. Ohtsuka was a classically trained martial artist with a teaching diploma in jiu jitsu. He incorporated jiu jitsu techniques into karate and founded his school, 'the way of peace', or *wado ryu*. Ohtsuka anticipated the development of karate as a combat sport and in 1929 he held the first ever karate competition.

These then are the four major schools (*ryu*) of karate. To recap, they are:

The SHOTOKAN, founded by Gichin Funakoshi
The GOJUKAI, founded by Chojun Miyagi
The SHITOKAI, founded by Kenwa Mabuni
The WADOKAI, founded by Hironori Ohtsuka

There are other schools but the Japanese rank them of lesser importance.

The side kick is a powerful penetrating technique.

KARATE STYLES

Much is made of the styles of karate. This is a pity in some ways because it promotes division and self-interest. When joining a karate club you will nevertheless encounter style, so it is as well if you know a little about it.

There is in fact not an enormous difference between the styles and such things as katas are common to several. There are differences however, in the way they are practised by different schools and it is not a good idea to mix them early on in your training.

As I mentioned earlier, there is no 'best' style of karate and you should beware clubs that try to tell you there is. Having said that, each style has certain characteristics which may suit some individuals more than others. If, for example, you are not interested in training for competition, then you would be better advised to join one of the associations which attach little importance to it.

Anyway, I have included some general characteristics of each major karate style for you to consider. Be warned though that not all styles are well represented throughout Britain and you may have to settle for an alternative to your first choice.

Shotokan

This is the style developed by Funakoshi himself. It is both powerful and well constructed, relying upon low, strong stances to receive and initiate attack. The techniques themselves are large in execution and there is extensive body coordination to ensure that maximum power is developed at the correct times. Importance is attached to what is called *kime* or 'focus'. This is the point in any technique where the maximum power and intent is developed. It is characterised by all the muscles of the body tensing, to make it as strong and as rigid as possible.

There are many katas and these are very deliberate and strongly executed, with grand movements, strong advances and powerful blocks. Competition is not over-emphasized but when practised, it is tough and uncompromising, scoring only those techniques which if uncontrolled, could be expected severely to injure the recipient.

Originally shotokan clubs did not allow sparring until the student had reached a high grade. This is a very sensible policy because medical evidence now shows quite clearly that the majority of injuries in karate occur when inexperienced karateka fight. However, most students want to start fighting as soon as possible and this policy has been subject to pressure.

Goju ryu

This style was originated by the Okinawan Chojun Miyagi. It is very traditional and competition plays a minor part. Unusually, goju ryu incorporates within it a fitness training programme designed to increase strength, endurance and speed. This programme uses specialised weights such as the weighted jar (which improves grip), the strength stones (which look like lollipops and strengthen the upper body) and the iron ring (which is used for general body building).

Core of the style is the stance known as *sanchin*. This is a very strong platform for resisting or responding to attacks. The centre of gravity is kept low and all power is developed from there – the upper body plays little part. This is the key to strong techniques and is available to all physiques. The semicircular step is much in evidence and there are circular strikes.

There are fewer katas to learn and by far the most important is sanchin. This is repeated whilst the instructor strikes certain muscles to determine whether they are in contraction. Having watched sanchin practised many times, I can see resemblances between it and the 'dynamic tension' method of body building developed by Charles Atlas. I think there is little doubt that continued practice of sanchin would develop muscle strength. This has been confirmed to me by senior karateka from other Okinawan schools.

Shito ryu

Shito ryu was originated by the Okinawan Kenwa Mabuni. In this one style are found the principal characteristics of all three major Okinawan karate categories. This is reflected in the enormous number of katas in the syllabus. On the whole, the movements tend to be shorter and crisper than shotokan, lighter and faster than those of goju ryu.

The style is much involved in competition worldwide but this is not to the detriment of its traditional karate content. The katas are particularly beautiful and incorporate an economy of movement and grace which is not seen in any of the other styles. Interestingly, shito ryu incorporates two katas which are customised but recognisable renderings of Southern Shaolin patterns. My personal opinion is that we will see an increase in the appearance of these older forms, much to the benefit of karate.

Wado ryu

Wado ryu, Ohtsuka's 'way of peace' was the style that I started in karate with. This was not by intent and I might well have taken up shotokan or one of the other styles; it was simply the first style I encountered. On reflection, I don't think it was too bad a choice!

Ohtsuka was Funakoshi's senior Japanese student and a noted Japanese martial artist in his own right. It was therefore inevitable that he would incorporate elements of his *budo* knowledge into karate. This he did to great effect, producing a graceful, fast style which relied rather more than other styles upon sophisticated evasion movements.

The style strenuously avoids direct confrontation with an opponent – a wise strategy if you are not over-imbued with physical strength. The strikes are typically fast, culminating in passive snapping movements.

Although drawing from the same pool of katas as shotokan, Ohtsuka gave them all older Chinese names. Thus shotokan's *heians* are wado ryu's *pinans*; *gankaku* is *chinto* and *hangetsu* is *seishan*.

There are fewer katas in the wado ryu syllabus than are found in shotokan's.

Like shito ryu, wado ryu students are successful in open competitions. Indeed it was Ohtsuka who pioneered karate competition.

Having spoken of the four major schools, I would now like to mention some of the other schools.

Like the Chinese martial arts, there are actually many styles of karate though some are little known outside the immediate circle of practitioners. Still others represent breakaways from one of 'the big four' mentioned above. There tends to be a clearly defined chain of authority from the founder of a style, down through each generation of students to the present day. Where this chain is not followed, then either new styles come into being, or two organisations practising the same style spring up.

The style known as *shukokai*, or more correctly *tani ha shitoryu* was founded by Chojiro Tani, the latter being a student of the shito ryu founder Kenwa Mabuni. When the mantle of authority passed to Mabuni's sons, Tani left to develop his own school.

Shukokai is a very scientific style of karate with much emphasis placed on the generation of maximum power in punches and kicks. In furtherance of this aim, techniques are delivered in a way that runs contrary to established practice. For example, the shukokai student is more concerned with soaking up the recoil of a successful technique by moving forward behind it rather than by using a static system of stance-bracing. The shukokai theory on effective stances makes a very interesting and convincing exposition.

Shotokai separated from the shotokan after Funakoshi's death. The shotokai felt that karate was moving too far from its original form and resolved to return to a more traditional way. Training is similar to shotokan but there is less emphasis on obvious focus and a more modular form of practice. There is no competition at all and only high grades are allowed to free spar.

Kyokushinkai, 'the way of ultimate truth' was founded by Masutatsu Oyama, the latter being a student of Funakoshi. Oyama disagreed with the format of shotokan practice and incorporated circular techniques and a particularly strenuous and potentially hazardous form of competition known as 'knockdown'.

There have been numerous other breakaways and there are at least two international organisations practising shotokan, and two practising wado ryu. Goju ryu suffered a split some years ago but that has now healed, so there is only one authentic international federation. Although there is only one authentic shito ryu in existence, there are several international organisations practising derivatives of it.

Under the circumstances, it is not surprising that these divisions persist up to national level. At the last count, there were more than 73 associations of clubs practising karate in England alone!

KARATE WEAPONS

As I mentioned earlier, karate was principally an armed combat system relying on hidden weapons. Okinawans were not allowed to carry swords or spears, so they developed their fighting systems around commonplace items such as the farmer's sickles, the flails for threshing rice, the handles from rice grinders, the quarter staff and the short threshing fork.

Usage of these weapons has all but vanished from karate, though the weapons themselves are popular as martial art 'badges'. A few schools teach students how to use these ancient weapons but I am sceptical as to whether they are shown properly. The rice flail for example, is twirled around in a manner which is purely decorative. The user seems more concerned with practising difficult swop-overs and flourishes than with using it as a weapon.

There has been a slight resurgence of interest in these weapons and their usage is being taught once more but whether in the traditional way or not I cannot say.

I would like to point something out before I move on.

Martial arts weapons are, as their name states – WEAPONS. The police can and do prosecute people carrying them around for no good reason. If you are stopped on your way to the training hall and have a flail in your training bag, it is less likely you will be prosecuted than if you are seen with it in a pub. So please use a little common sense when carrying them.

Kama

Kama are the sickles used by the Okinawan farmer or labourer. Typically they consist of stout wooden handles with shallow curved and exceedingly sharp blades. Kama are normally used in pairs and can hook, cut, slash and bludgeon.

Ton fa

The *ton fa*, sometimes called *tui fa* are the handles which slotted into the tops of the circular rice grinder wheels. They consist of a strong wooden baton with a peg-like handle sticking up from one end. When held by the peg, they can be swung so the baton swivels out, or used to shield the forearm during a block. They give a useful extension to a punch when held parallel to the lower arm.

Some people claim that ton fa could stop a Japanese sword but I have reason to doubt this after seeing one inadvertently sliced in two by a sword during a staged demonstration!

Rokushakubo

The *rokushakubo* is the six foot staff common to many nations. The Okinawan staff was made of dense native wood, polished smooth with tapering ends to discourage the opponent from grasping it. Okinawans tended to use the staff as an extension of the natural body movements. This meant it could be employed in restricted spaces.

Many moves seen in modern karate are based upon the staff.

Nun chaku

Nun chaku or 'rice flails' are common agricultural implements found throughout South East Asia. Normally they consist of two heavy batons joined by a flap of leather at their ends. The flail adapted for martial arts usage uses either a thong or a chain to join the batons. The flails can be swung at the opponent, or the link used to entrap them.

Flails are difficult to use and can cause injury to the inexperienced user.

Sais

Sais are short threshing forks used in pairs. They are pointed metal batons with a forward curving finger guard that makes them look a little like tridents. With a little practice they can be thrown short distances but were normally used to thump people with the blunt end. They could also be used to deflect attacks by other Okinawan weapons.

KARATE AND THE LAW

Thanks to the antics of Bruce Lee and David Carradine, the oriental martial arts have an undeserved reputation for equipping their followers with the most extraordinary powers. If you ever read the newspapers, you will notice that any martial artist in the news is a 'karate expert'. There seem to be no karate students!

I have lost count of the times I have been called to give evidence in a court case where a young lad has been prosecuted by the police for having two pieces of broom handle attached, through the elegant if precarious medium of bent nails, by a piece of old lavatory chain. When all is said and done, this remains no more than two bits of stick poorly fastened together; yet courts persist in viewing it as being as dangerous as a brick in a sock!

The martial artist faced with a situation where he or she may have to fight is at a distinct disadvantage. Such is the martial art reputation that the courts found a young karate black belt guilty of causing actual bodily harm to two amateur boxers who attacked him! The court felt that his martial art knowledge made him somehow different.

So the moral is clear! If you study karate, avoid fights outside the training hall like the plague. Walk away from insults and do not respond to threatening behaviour.

People with convictions for crimes of violence should disclose them to the club instructor. It does not automatically mean you will be disbarred. The MAC has produced a set of guidelines to help the instructor assess each case individually. The club is only likely to deny membership if the instructor feels that you still have a propensity towards violence, or where your occupation (i.e. nightclub bouncer) makes you likely routinely to employ karate techniques for violent purposes.

One thing is certain and that is that if you don't disclose a conviction and it is found out later, the club instructor may disbar you.

CHOOSING THE RIGHT KARATE CLUB

Choosing the right karate club is the most important step you will take in your karate career. Pick the wrong one and you could waste many years of hard practice!

Not all karate clubs are good clubs. There are those where the instructor is poorly qualified and has a low standard. I personally know of two national associations with impressive sounding names. One gave a black belt to a dog and the other, a teaching diploma to a person who'd never done a day's martial art in his life!

A karate instructor can produce the most impressive looking certificates to demonstrate how qualified he or she is. I always remember one, apparently in Japanese, that was sent to me for checking. I had it translated and found that it was an extract from a Chinese takeaway menu!

I know of other associations run by instructors who left Japan as first dan black belts and arrived in Britain as fourth dans!

There is no legal requirement, as there is in France, for karate instructors to be recognised by a national body. Despite this, many of Britain's top karateka have organised themselves into governing bodies which set out to establish proper standards of qualification and behaviour. So successful have these been that their efforts have been recognised by such bodies as the British Olympic Association and the Central Council for Physical Recreation.

When it was found that to escape the net, some karate instructors were claiming to teach other martial arts, the British Karate Control Commission led a move to form an all-embracing Martial Arts Commission. The Commission, or 'MAC' as it is commonly called, consists of the governing bodies for all the major martial arts practised in Britain. Regardless of whether they are karate, kung fu, taekwondo – whatever – they have agreed to operate proper standards. You can recognise any MAC affiliated club because it issues MAC licences.

MAC licences look like credit cards. They have the holder's

name, whether an instructor or a student, the martial art practised and an expiry date. Particularly useful is the insurance policy they contain. This indemnifies the holder against both personal accident risk and against injuring a third party.

MAC instructors are the only people to take national coaching courses approved by both the governing body and the National Coaching Foundation. As a result, they are able to teach more effectively and safely than non-certificated instructors.

If you join an MAC-recognised club, your grades will be recognised nationally and if you are interested in competition, you may well stand a chance to represent your country at international competitions!

To find out the address of your local MAC recognised club, call the Martial Arts Commission on 01 691 3433, or write enclosing a stamped addressed envelope to:

> The Martial Arts Commission,
> 1st Floor Broadway House,
> 15–16 Deptford Broadway,
> London SE8 4PE.

Newspapers are full of martial art clubs advertising for new members. Before taking the plunge, look to see whether the words 'MAC recognised' appear anywhere. MAC clubs are generally proud of their recognition and like to advertise the fact. Watch out for clubs that use a lot of hype, such as 'best', 'biggest', 'strongest' etc. These claims are nearly always false.

WHAT WILL IT COST?

Most karate clubs are run by the instructor; few are run by a committee of the membership. Some are limited companies. The club is in membership of an association and the association itself is in direct or indirect membership of a governing body.

When you join a karate club, you will either pay one fee which encompasses all of these various affiliations, or you will pay a series of smaller ones. The club fee registers you as a member of that club. In many cases, it also includes an application for the MAC licence which I mentioned earlier. Although the cost of an MAC licence is scarcely more than a couple of pounds, the association may decide to surcharge it, to gain revenue for promoting its own activities.

Having joined the club and its parent association, you will be automatically issued with an MAC licence within 31 days of joining. This will come in a licence book that serves to record your personal progress within the association. Don't worry about insurance during the 31 days because if you have paid your monies immediately upon joining, then the club officer will have notified the association HQ of your membership and you will be indemnified.

Whatever you do, make sure you apply for your MAC licence immediately upon joining. Don't be fobbed off because accidents tend to happen more frequently in the early days of training and that is when you need your insurance the most.

Each time you train, you may be required to pay a mat fee. This varies from a few pence to a couple of pounds. Average length of a session is ninety minutes and it is usual to train at least twice a week. Sessions of more than ninety minutes tend to run you out of steam, whereas less than that is insufficient to qualify you for gradings within a reasonable time.

At some stage, you will need to buy a karate suit, or *karategi* to give it the correct name. Try to put off buying one for as long as possible because you may find karate is not, after all, to your liking and a second-hand karate suit is difficult to re-sell at a reasonable price.

Most clubs can supply you with a suit cheaper than the price you would pay if you went to a normal sports shop. Alternatively you can go to a specialist martial arts shop. There are usually three qualities of suit offered. The cheapest is a lightweight suit; then there is a medium weight and finally a heavyweight tournament suit. If you can afford it, go for the medium weight. This lasts longer and looks nicer.

Always buy one size too large and wash it before you wear it because regardless of what the manufacturer claims, suits always shrink every time they are washed. For the first few lessons you may look a bit like the Cutty Sark in full sail on a windy day but in a month or so, it will shrink to a good fit. It is important to have a lot of free play in the thigh and groin area because you must be able to lift your knee high without the material pulling.

Every forty-eight hours of training, you will be eligible to take a grading. The latter is a form of examination to see what standard you have reached in your techniques. If you are successful, you will be upgraded and allowed to wear a different coloured belt. Although the number of grades and belt colours vary, the following is a common scheme:

> Red or white belt
> White belt
> Yellow belt
> Orange belt
> Green belt
> Purple belt
> Brown belt (3 grades)
> Black belt

Some associations award each grade first, second, or third class. Second class is an average pass, third is a skin-of-the-teeth and first is a good pass. Exceptional students may miss out a grade altogether and jump into the next.

Grading fees vary tremendously and are sometimes charged at different rates for the grade taken. The new belt costs a few pounds and can be bought through the club, or from a sports shop. Judo belts are quite acceptable. One thing though; don't be tempted to dye your old belt to the new colour. With the sweat of training, the dye always runs and colours your karate suit.

There is a right and a wrong way to tie a belt. Start by wrapping the belt twice around your waist (*fig 1*). Tuck one end up the inside of both coils (*fig 2*) and bring it over the top (*fig 3*).

Figure 1

Figure 2

Figure 3

Figure 4

Figure 5

Bring the second end across and tuck the first under and through it (*fig 4*), pulling the knot tight (*fig 5*). If you have succeeded, the belt ends will be of equal length and protruding from either side of the knot.

If you enter a competition, you will have to pay a small fee but if representing your club, then expect the latter to pay for you. Make sure that your MAC licence is up to date before you take part in either a competition or a grading. It is not the association's responsibility to notify you (though some do), when your licence expires.

ETIQUETTE

One of the things I like best about karate is the etiquette. It is that which sets it apart from other physical activities. A cornerstone of good karate practice is respect; respect for the teacher and for the other students. Even the place of training, or *dojo* as it is known, is treated with respect in the good karate club. Even if no-one is in the dojo when you enter, pause at the entrance and face the centre of the room. Put your heels together and your hands flat against the front of your thighs and bow (*fig 6*).

Don't bow too far, just incline your upper body forward. Make the bow smooth and hesitate for a count of two at the lowest point. The name of this formal attention stance is *kaisoku dachi* and it is adopted whenever the command "*Nori!*" is called.

Figure 6

As befits the follower of any true fighting art, you should always be on the lookout for attack so never look at the floor.

Let me tell you about a keen Japanese martial artist I once met. He was descended from a warrior family and believed he should observe the dictates of martial art teaching at all times. Thus he always slept on his front with his hand over his heart, in case someone came to stab him whilst he was asleep. He always sat facing the entrance of a room – never with his back to it. Everywhere he went, he automatically searched out the possible avenues of escape, should he be ambushed. This is an extreme example. The last thing I would suggest is that you get into the habit of suddenly spinning around as you walk, to see whether anyone is sneaking up behind you. The object is a realistic increase in your awareness of potentially hazardous situations. The good karateka will use awareness to avoid getting into a situation where a fight is necessary.

Anyway, to return to the bow; once you have made it, step into the training hall. Bow too when leaving the hall, even if for a short interval. If someone is already in the training hall, bow towards that person. If more than one, choose the person with the highest grade as shown by belt colour and bow to them. If you arrive after the class has started, do not just walk in. Exercise first and if required, perform two kneeling bows as described a little later. Then stand or kneel conspicuously at the edge of the mat and wait to be called on by the class senior.

It is as well at this point, to learn some of the terms you may come across in the training hall. The club instructor is correctly addressed as *Sensei* and any student senior to yourself as *Sempai*. Students of lower grade are referred to as *Kohei*. Bow to your classmates as well as to the instructor, since it is they you will be learning with.

Behaviour in the training hall identifies the true karateka. Don't talk noisily or lark about. If you sit down, cross your legs so no-one will trip over them. It is the height of bad manners to smoke, or sprawl out on the floor. When standing, don't lounge against walls.

At the beginning of the training session you will be called to order. The class lines up in grade lines, so make sure the person in front of you has the same colour belt as you have. Tidy your karate suit and check your belt is properly fastened. Adopt attention stance and wait quietly. When the class is settled, the senior will call "*Seiza!*" Drop onto your right knee, keeping your hands to your sides (*fig 7*). Bring your left knee down, alongside the first (*fig 8*). Point your toes, then sit down onto your calves. Keep your back straight and hold your head up (*fig 9*). This position can be painful at first, especially for older students, so practise it at home on a carpet or cushion until you get used to it.

Figure 7

Figure 8

Figure 9

Figure 10

The class bows to the teacher on the command "*Sensei ni rei!*"
Slide both palms forward and off your knees. Incline your upper
body into a low bow, making sure you can still see the person in
front (*fig 10*). Don't look at the floor and pause for two seconds
at the lowest part before returning to an upright position. When
the senior calls "*Otagai ni rei!*" perform a second kneeling bow,
this time intended for your classmates.

Sometimes – usually at the end of a session when this sequence is repeated, the senior will call "*Mokuso!*" When this
happens, close your eyes and meditate until stopped by the
command "*Mokuso yamei!*"

When the senior calls "*Kiritsu!*", lift your left knee, then your
right and straighten into a standing position with your heels
pressed together, feet slightly splayed and hands resting on the
forward/outer quadrant of your thighs (*fig 11*). At no time whilst
getting up should you raise your heel clear of the floor and rest
on the ball of your foot (*fig 12*). If someone were to step on your
foot in that position, it could be very injurious.

If your belt becomes unfastened at any time, drop onto one
knee and re-tie it. If people are moving up behind you in class
lines, use your common sense and step out of the line to avoid
getting run into or tripped over.

When the instructor is showing the class a technique, make
sure you can see the demonstration clearly. If you are chosen to
assist the instructor, don't make fatuous remarks or move about
unbidden. When training with a partner, avoid loud discussion
and speak only when there is a need to; then keep it short.

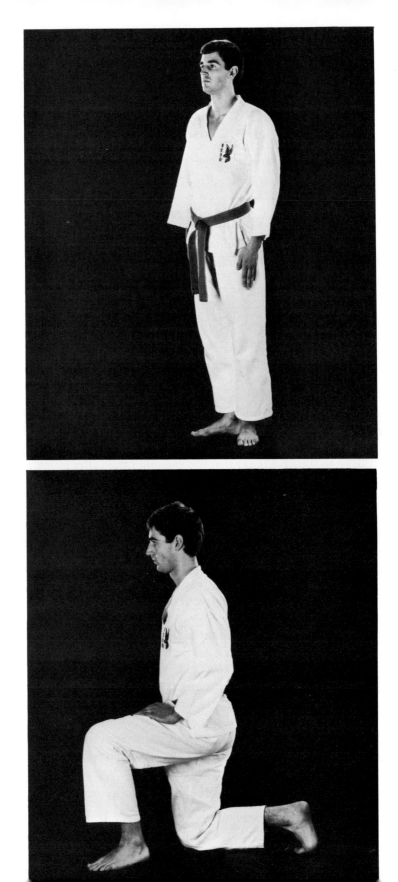

Figure 11

Figure 12

SOME SAFETY HINTS

Karate can be quite a strenuous activity, especially for someone coming into it cold from a sedentary job. Hard training places quite severe demands on the body and the instructor is unlikely to slow the whole class down to suit the least fit member. Therefore check whether you're fit enough to practise.

Having said that, the demands it places are not out of the ordinary and if you do other things like swimming or squash, you will be able to cope with karate. If you don't do any form of exercising, then I would advise you to take up a fitness improvement scheme. If you don't, you will spend your lessons gasping for breath and trying just to last through the session rather than concentrating on improving technique.

I won't go into exercise programmes at this point but will cover them a little later. I will also refer to diet in the section on fitness, so suffice it to say that you shouldn't train after eating a large meal. This is because the process of digestion uses up a lot of blood which is otherwise required in the exercising muscles – including the heart – and cramp may result.

Make sure that the club instructor knows if you suffer from any complaint likely to affect your ability to train. I can only think of one condition that would disqualify you out of hand and that is haemophilia. Even if you suffer from von Willebrandt's Disease or sarcoidosis you may still be allowed to train by your doctor.

Asthmatics are likely to improve through training and I have known many who got their black belts without problem. Just make sure you keep your medication where you can reach it at all times. The same comments apply to diabetics. Keep some lemonade in your training bag. Even a heart condition is no bar to training if you keep within limits and get clearance from your doctor. As a matter of fact I know someone with a cardiac condition who has been training now for more than ten years without mishap. Since starting karate, he has been able to give up medication (with his doctor's approval, of course).

If the instructor knows about your health condition, he/she can check your performance and may spot the onset of symptoms before you do.

If you suffer from knee, elbow, or low back problems, you may find karate is not helpful. There is some evidence to suggest that badly taught karate actually causes these complaints! People who suffer from arthritic conditions are similarly at risk and should take medical advice before starting karate.

Certain types of virus infections can have serious side effects on heart muscle and so you should avoid sharp bangs on the chest and sudden training spurts if you have a cold.

It would be silly to pretend that accidents are unknown in karate. Like any boisterous activity, bumps and bruises can and do occur. The most common 'injuries' encountered are blisters on the soles of the feet before they get used to the barefooted scuffing around. Take a little first aid pack with you in your training bag. This should include something to clean skin surfaces – like the baby-bottom wipes you can buy from chemists. Include also some sticking plasters. A crepe bandage has little actual value but it is a comforting placebo to wrap around a bruised shin or twisted ankle.

I now want to mention something about the training hall itself. Since few clubs are rich enough to have custom-made training halls, most have to rely on church halls or local authority general purpose rooms. Sometimes these have unsuitable floors.

Overly deep mats can cause wrenches to the knee joint and ankles, whilst mats which move about can catch your foot or toe. Since karate involves much tooing and froing, there is always a risk you will get dumped on the floor at some stage or another. A stone floor can be pretty inhospitable to land on with the back of your head, so bear this in mind.

The ideal surface is one that is non-slip and has a slight resilience, or 'give' to it, such as sprung wooden floors.

FIT TO TRAIN

Being involved as I have been, with martial artists of all disciplines, I have come into contact with a great many theories on fitness and health. Some of these are western based, the others are oriental. The two often complement each other quite well.

People of all shapes and sizes can practise karate. Very fat people may experience some problems with the flexibility requirements simply because flab can inhibit the amount of movement at a joint. Despite this, some fat people are extremely strong and can move with surprising speed.

Eastern notions of medicine and fitness lie in a different direction to those of the west. Western medicine treats a specific complaint whilst eastern medicine treats the whole body. The eastern viewpoint is that if the body is healthy, illness will not develop. There is much to be said for this viewpoint and nowadays more people than ever are becoming aware of the need to maintain a healthy body.

To get the best from your training you should try and follow a whole-body, whole-life regimen. Eat frequent small meals and never close to a training session. Try to eliminate fat from your diet as far as possible. One of the ways of doing this is to reduce your red meat intake. Take chicken and fish instead. If you must use sugar, then use only the unrefined variety. Eat plenty of wholefoods and avoid tinned or preserved foods wherever possible.

To cope with a karate class, you should build up your stamina. Stamina depends in part upon the efficiency of your lungs to capture oxygen and your bloodstream to transport that oxygen to the working muscles. Waste products must be equally efficiently siphoned out of the muscle before they build up and block its function.

Achieve an improvement here by making the pumping efficiency of your heart muscle more efficient through a gradually increasing workload. The heart is no more than a bag of muscle and like all muscles, if it isn't exercised enough, it becomes flabby and loses efficiency. Exercise it by increasing the speed at which it pumps and holding that increase for at least fifteen minutes. Do this three times a week minimum and as you find it easier to manage, extend the period of exercise to thirty minutes.

The kind of exercises which do this are jogging, swimming, or cycling.

Certain muscles are used more than others during training and these can be separately worked by a series of specialised exercises. Assuming that specialist equipment is not readily available, concentrate on building up major muscle groups by exercises such as the following.

Press-ups are very good for developing upper body strength. Women find them difficult but if they cannot manage even one, then if they sink down on their knees (*fig 13*), they will find them easier. Always maintain a straight back during press-ups. Students either hinge in the middle and poke their backsides in the air, or they sag until their bellies touch the floor. These are bad habits which reduce the value of the exercise.

Lock your arms straight and have them shoulder-width apart.

Figure 13

Figure 14

Look forward, not at the ground. Lower yourself down until your chest brushes the floor (*fig 14*), then drive your body back up by straightening your arms. Do at least ten press-ups, gradually improving over the weeks until you can manage fifty at any one session.

A good variation on press-ups for strengthening the triceps is to start with the hands overlying each other (*fig 15*). Drop your body down on to your elbows (*fig 16*), and using only the power of your arms, push your body clear of the ground. Once this becomes easy, place your hands well forward of your head to increase muscle loadings.

Figure 15

Figure 16

Keep with the press-up position for a little longer but this time poke your backside up and back as far as possible, (*fig 17*). Pause at the highest position, then curve your body down and forwards between your elbows, allowing your chest to brush the floor (*fig 18*). Allow your arms to straighten, so your back arches and your stomach hangs down (*fig 19*). Push your shoulders

Figure 17

Figure 18

Figure 19

back, your bottom up and repeat the sequence. This is an excellent exercise for loosening the back.

From press-up position, drop your body until you are lying flat on your front. Curl your feet back and catch your ankles with your hands (*fig 20*). Try and arch your back as far as you can (*fig 21*) and hold for a count of ten before releasing. Be careful because this exercise can cause you to black out! Repeat the exercise five times, with suitable rest periods between each.

Figure 20

Figure 21

Then roll onto your back and draw up your knees. Clasp your hands behind your head (*fig 22*). Arch your body up as far as you can and if possible, touch your forehead against your knees (*fig 23*). Do this at least twenty times. Because I have a heavy upper body, I find this difficult to do and my feet keep coming off the ground. I counter this by hooking my feet under something.

Figure 22

Figure 23

Figure 24

Figure 25

When you can do this exercise well, try rotating your trunk as you roll up so you touch your knees with the diagonal elbow (*figs 24 & 25*).

Legs can be strengthened by a variety of means but you should avoid bending the knees beyond ninety degrees under load.

Begin by standing on one leg whilst extending the other straight in front of you (*fig 26*). Keep your arms to your side and slowly lower your body until there is a ninety degree bend in the knee joint (*fig 27*). Hold this for a count of five and slowly straighten. Repeat this exercise five times and then change legs. If you find difficulty keeping your balance, take hold of something to steady you (*fig 28*).

Figure 26

Figure 27

Figure 28

To make a blitz on endurance, set yourself a circuit to train on. This should mix different exercises, each of which is repeated a set number of times before going on to the next. Start with a few repetitions of each and aim to finish the circuit within a pre-set time. If you finish on time, begin gradually increasing the number of repetitions. This kind of training is exhausting and only really necessary when you are training up for a grading or a competition.

Speed is very important because it is no good developing tremendous strength with a technique if it is recognised and avoided. Build up speed in the arms by punching in fast repetitions. Don't bother about power, or in locking the arms straight, just pump them out as quickly as possible. If you have access to equipment, pull back your punch against the tension of a spring and then punch with the spring as quickly as possible. Make sure the spring doesn't over-extend your elbow otherwise it will injure the joint.

You can also hold a light weight in your fist as you punch but don't let your elbow slam straight.

Leg speed can be increased by sprinting on the spot, lifting your knees as high and as fast as you can. Another good exercise is running forwards and backwards in sand or in water. If neither is available, run up a hill as quickly as possible, then sprint down.

The part of karate which defeats most people is the flexibility requirement. Many styles of karate use quite high kicks – sometimes to the opponent's head. This requires fair flexibility in the legs. As with endurance, there are specific types of exercises to increase flexibility and I want to deal with a few at this point.

It is always a good idea to do the other exercises first, so when you start stretching, the joints have been well exercised. Flexibility is limited by the length of the muscle which operates the joint. The muscle is inserted into either side of the joint by inelastic fibres of the tendons. Any stretching force applied to the muscle must not fall upon the tendons but upon the bulk of the muscle itself. As you stretch, feel for where the maximum pull is occurring. It should always be in the centre of the muscle; if it isn't, take a close look at the way you are doing your exercise.

There will come a point during the stretch when you start to feel pain. Gradually approach this threshold – don't suddenly jerk up to it. When you reach it, hold the stretch for a count of ten, then relax. Always try to exceed your previous limits. One way to do this is by approaching the threshold, then without lessening the stretch, tighten up all your muscles – especially the one being stretched – as tightly as you can. Hold this contraction for a count of at least five, then relax and continue the stretch. You will generally find that this gives an extra couple of inches' movement.

Start with a gentle hamstring stretch by pushing hard against a wall (*fig 29*). Keep your back leg straight and don't allow the knee to bend. Your heel must remain firmly pressed to the floor.

Figure 29

Follow this with a gentle open stretch. Spread your legs apart and lower your weight slowly and assymetrically onto the left. Keep the soles of both feet pressed to the floor and support your weight by resting your palms on your knees (*fig 30*). Push down on the extended leg and hold for a count of five. Then smoothly shift your weight so it comes to lie over the other leg (*fig 31*). Repeat the exercise for at least five sets.

Figure 30

Figure 31

Figure 32

Figure 33

Next extend the stretch by sinking down on one leg whilst fully extending the other (*fig 32*). Drop your bottom down as low as you can get it and hold this lowest position for a count of five. Keeping the body low, swing across so weight comes to overlie the other leg (*fig 33*) and repeat.

Figure 34

Sit down on the floor with the soles of your feet together. Pull them until the heels are near your groin and hold the ankles. Try and push your knees down (*fig 34*). This exercise can be improved with the aid of a partner who applies a gradually increasing pressure on the knees. Don't allow your partner to jerk down nor to exceed your capability.

Figure 35

Stretch your hamstrings and your back by extending your legs out straight in front. Take hold of the balls of your feet and try to drag the heels off the floor, leaning forwards as you do (*fig 35*). A variation of this uses a diagonal lift to the leg being stretched. Whilst sitting, take your foot in the opposite hand (*fig 36*) and then extend it up and away from your body, so it locks straight (*fig 37*). Hold the straightened leg for a count of five, then change legs.

Figure 36

Figure 37

Figure 38

Figure 39

Figure 40

Finally open your legs as wide as they will go, keeping the backs of your knees pressed to the floor. Lean forward and stretch out with both hands, keeping the palms just off the floor (*fig 38*). Look forward not down and sweep your hands from side to side in gentle arcs (*figs 39 & 40*). Maintain this exercise for a minimum count of twenty.

I started this chapter talking about eastern concepts of health and fitness and I will finish in the same vein by describing meditation. Meditation is a part of the process needed for your body to react correctly and without conscious thought.

As I have previously said, you can meditate effectively whilst practising but it is best to set aside a little time to do it properly.

Begin by taking up a comfortable position. I prefer sitting straightbacked in a chair. A friend prefers to sit cross-legged on the floor whilst another prefers to stand. Whichever you choose, try and relax but keep your back straight (*fig 41*). Trying to still your mind is very difficult. If you erect a mental thought shield, you spend so much effort maintaining it that it becomes impossible to relax! Therefore try to divert your attention. The method I use is to envisage that I am floating in cold dark water. I try to feel the water moving around me and imagine its wetness. This has the effect of calming my mind for limited periods of time.

Figure 41

PRE-TRAINING

Considering the way the hands and feet are used in karate, I am amazed how little time is devoted to training them to equal the task. The front punch, for example, is a mainstay of karate at all levels, yet beyond a couple of minutes at the beginning of my first karate lesson I was never shown how to make my fist into an effective weapon. After six months of flailing away with it at the air, I struck my first opponent and skinned my knuckles!

It could have been worse; my wrist could have folded on impact and sprained.

Therefore my advice to you is to develop your hands and feet so they are capable of doing what karate demands of them. Unless you join a shukokai or goju ryu club, you won't get enough practice in the lesson, so it will fall to you to practise at home.

If you are a real red-toothed karate fanatic, make yourself a punching post or *makiwara*. But if you want to retain the natural shape of your hands, make do with a punching pad.

To make a makiwara, take an eight foot length of springy hardwood and shape it so the bottom four feet are four inches by four inches and the top four feet taper evenly to four inches by two. Then sink the bottom four feet into your garden, preferably anchoring it with concrete. Get hold of a piece of hard rubber, such as is used for conveyor belts or industrial flooring and glue six inches of it to the top of the wider surface of the post.

In Japanese books you are advised to use rice straw for the impact area but not only will you find difficulty in getting this, you will also find it cannot be kept together in use. An additional disadvantage is that it cannot be kept clean and may cause infections to scuffed skin surfaces.

The makiwara is used to develop a good fist. The latter shows a ninety degree bend in the big knuckle joints, so the middle finger joints are kept out of the way. The average person can't make the fist tight enough, so these lower joints protrude and get painfully barked on impact.

Below the roots of your fingers at the top of your palm is a ridge formed by the underside of the large knuckles. Fold your fingers down so their tips contact it (*figs 42 & 43*), then close the

Figure 42

Figure 43

Figure 44

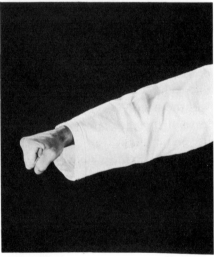

Figure 45

fist fully and lock the fingers in by folding your thumb across the index and middle fingers (*figs 44 & 45*).

Don't let your thumb poke forward or it will catch in someone's sleeve and do not enclose it by the fingers, or it will be damaged when your fist strikes something hard.

Most of the time, your fist can be slightly relaxed but always tighten it fully on impact.

If you are right handed, stand to the left of and facing the makiwara with your left foot leading. Raise your right arm and gently punch the makiwara, keeping your thumb turned inwards and the back of your wrist upwards. Do not punch quickly or hard, since you will bruise your knuckles, but do drive your punch into the pad so it bends. When you have done a comfortable number of repetitions, change your stance and repeat the exercise using the left fist.

You will find that, because the knuckles of your fist do not all lie in one line, you will only be able to land some of them on the pad – not all. Karate uses the index and middle knuckles only, so aim your fist so these alone contact the pad. Because the middle knuckle protrudes further than the others, it is all too easy to land on it alone. This can prove painful to the unconditioned fist. As you punch, keep your forearm in line with the back of your fist to stop the wrist from folding on impact.

If you work on the pad each day for fifteen minutes, your fist will soon be able to withstand a hard impact. Provided you do not hammer the pad, your knuckles will not deform, apart from some redness and slightly thickened skin. Keen karateka however may wish to go at it with more enthusiasm and so should increase the force of impact gradually over a long period. This causes the skin over the knuckles to thicken and if not cared for properly, it will split and become scarred. Some people regard this as they do a faded belt – as a mark of honour.

If the skin does split, clean the abrasions with hot brine and leave off practice until new skin has formed. If the knuckles become bruised, stop training, unless of course, you actually want hypertrophied knuckle joints that click every time you flex your fingers.

Karateka below the age of eighteen years should not regularly use a makiwara because it can damage the growing ends of bones and produce serious deformities.

Next train the palm of your hand on the makiwara. First form the weapon by extending your hand out, then folding the fingers down to the palm-base. Lock your thumb into the side of your palm and bend your wrist back (*fig 46*). Stand as for the front punch and strike the pad with the base of your palm, keeping your folded fingers back out of harm's way and angling your forearm so as to present the correct part of the palm to the pad.

Use the makiwara also to develop knife hand strike, making the weapon by extending your fingers out and locking the thumb across the palm (*fig 47*). Keep your fingers locked straight or they will rattle painfully together on impact.

Stand sideways-on to the makiwara – your right side closest to it if you are right handed. Raise your right knife hand and bring

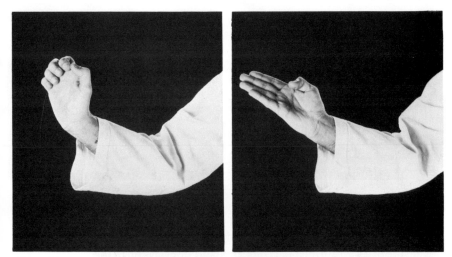

Figure 46

Figure 47

Figure 48

it across your chest so it nearly cups your left ear, palm turned towards your face. Twist your hips and upper body away from the pad. Beginning from the hips, swivel back towards the pad, letting your shoulders follow and swinging your hand into the pad. As it is about to make contact, rotate your hand palm down and land on the edge of the palm between the wrist and base of little finger.

Next practise the technique called 'ridge hand'. Make knife hand as before but force your thumb further across the palm (*fig 48*). This time impact is made with the thumb-side of the hand, using the bone of the index knuckle. Stand as for knife strike and if you are right handed, begin with your left leg closest to the makiwara, striking the pad with a short, palm-down swinging action. If you impact at too sharp an angle, you will bend your fingers back painfully. If the angle is too flat, you will land with your wrist bone.

Figure 49   Figure 50

The next hand technique to practise is perhaps the easiest. It is called 'hammerfist' and uses the pad of flesh under the little finger side of a well-formed fist (*fig 49*). Stand sideways on to the makiwara with your right foot next to it. Wind your body back and rotate your fist until the palm is near your left ear, exactly as you did for knife hand. Swing into the pad, striking it firmly.

Back fist also uses a fist but impact is made with the backs – not the fronts – of the two large knuckles (*fig 50*). Stand as for hammer fist, but don't rotate your forearm on impact. Strike the pad with the wrist turned slightly so the back of your wrist will be protected from impact.

'Back hand' uses the back of the hand to impact on target (*fig 51*). The hand configuration is as for knife hand, with fingers straight and thumb tucked in. Stand sideways to the post and bring your right palm to your left ear as for knife hand. When you swing it in to strike the pad, don't rotate the forearm, striking with the back of your hand only.

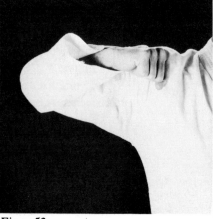

Figure 51   Figure 52

Because the makiwara is so springy, I don't like using it for elbow strikes (*fig 52*). A heavy suspended bag is better. If you nevertheless want to use the makiwara, stand facing it with your left foot leading as for front punch. Fold your right arm up and behind you, clenching your hand into a firm fist. Turn your hips into the pad and swing your shoulders behind them, allowing the point of your elbow to strike the pad. Provided you have made a good fist and the thumb-side is facing your chest, you won't hit your funny-bone.

The impact pad of a makiwara is very small, so I never use it for improving kicks. A real impact pad is much more suitable.

An impact pad consists of several layers of a special plastic foam much stiffer than that you normally see used for stuffing. It is called 'closed cell plastazote foam' and is available in sheets of around one and a half inches thickness. Use an electric knife to carve it into eighteen inch squares and hold as many as five pieces together by tying an old karate belt around them.

Pads can also be bought from martial arts supply shops, already enclosed in a tough, easily cleaned plastic cover. This has straps attached to the back, allowing you to hold it as you want (*figs 53 & 54*).

Figure 53   *Figure 54*

To use the pad effectively requires the assistance of a partner. It can be hung on a wall but that is less satisfactory. The foam removes all likelihood of causing bruises to the person holding it, yet shock is readily transmitted and you can see exactly how much force your technique develops against a man-mass.

Use the pad for all the exercises described above and you will find it less punishing to the hands. Use it also for kicks but check your partner is holding it firmly enough. Since kicks are powerful, it is better if your partner holds it against his/her left shoulder, steadying it by means of the strap.

Ball of foot kicks use the thick pad of flesh that runs beneath the toes. Because of the walking we do, this part of the foot is already well cushioned and needs little actual conditioning. What is needed though is practice at getting the foot into the correct configuration – beginners tend to land either with the toes or flat of the foot, neither of which is correct.

The first configuration is used in front kick. Point your foot

Figure 55

in a straight line with your shin and pull your toes back. It is sometimes difficult to get this correct so practise by placing the sole of your foot flat on the floor, then raise the heel as high as you can. Once you can adopt this foot position, try it out against the impact pad. Begin by getting the pad at a suitable height and don't be tempted into having it held too high.

Practise ball of foot kicks by standing with your left foot in front of the right, both knees slightly bent. Bring your right knee up and forwards until it is pointing at the pad (*fig 55*), then kick out with the lower leg, so the ball of your foot strikes the pad (*fig 56*). Bring your foot back smartly afterwards. If you hit the pad at the correct angle, your foot will dig into it. If not your foot will tend to skate up the front of the pad. Practise kicking on both legs and aim for penetration. As you become more proficient, go for harder and harder impacts but always withdraw your foot fully after the kick before putting it back down.

Figure 56

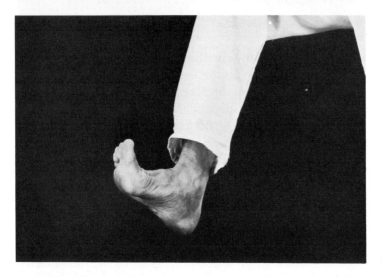

Figure 57

The second configuration for ball of foot has the toes pulled back as before, but the sole of the foot is now at right angles to the shin – as it is when standing normally (*fig 57*). Stand to the side of the impact pad and swing your bent knee up and out to the side (*fig 58*). Swivel on your supporting leg so you turn sideways on to the pad (*fig 59*) and when your knee is facing it, strike with the lower part of your foot. As in front kick, try to get good penetration of the pad and withdraw the kick after delivery, setting it down carefully.

Figure 58

Figure 59

The second type of foot weapon is the instep, with foot fully extended and in line with the shin, the toes turned downwards. Impact is made just in front of the ankle. Avoid striking with the base of the toes as this can be extremely painful. Use as for the turning ball of foot kick described above (*fig 60*).

Figure 60

Figure 61   Figure 62

The third type uses the heel of the foot. Stand with your back
to the pad and right foot leading (*fig 61*). Pick up your right foot
and pull your toes back, drawing it back to your left thigh (*fig
62*), and driving it heel-first into the impact pad (*fig 63*). Keep
looking at the pad throughout and lean away from the kick to
preserve your balance. After impact, withdraw your foot and set
it down carefully.

Figure 63

Figure 64

Turn so your left side faces the pad and raise your left foot until the knee is at the same height as the pad. Keep the sole of your foot parallel to the floor whilst raising your big toe and turning down all the others (*fig 64*). Drive your heel out sideways into the impact pad and at the same time, twist your supporting leg away from the direction of the kick (*fig 65*). As with back kick, lean away from the kick and conclude it by withdrawing the leg close to your body (*fig 66*).

Figure 65
(*below left*)

Figure 66
(*below right*)

Figure 67

The final foot weapon to condition is the inner edge of the foot, below the big toe. Get your partner to step forward on the left leg and lay the impact pad alongside the shin. Stand with your left foot forwards, swing your right leg in a curving motion low off the floor and strike the pad with the sole of your foot. Make as though to scoop your partner's left leg off the ground (*fig 67*). Swivel your body behind the swing whilst keeping your face back out of reprisal range.

POWERFUL TECHNIQUES

Provided you have developed the weapons of your hands and feet properly, then you have a number of fairly substantial bludgeons. As a friend of mine often remarks, "You don't need to do more than to tap someone in the face with a sledgehammer to do mischief!"

Each of us is limited in the amount of impact we can generate with our punches and kicks. The object of power training is to raise impact force to the maximum that we can realistically achieve. However, I would like to point out that the bigger you are, the greater potential you have for generating impact. Smaller people are forced to rely more upon accurate targetting of techniques and skill in distancing, timing and evasion.

When trying to generate power, techniques must be delivered as quickly as possible because as everyone knows, acceleration multiplied by mass equals force of impact. Before we get into simple newtonian physics, I want to spend a couple of lines telling you how to get an immediate benefit from any technique you use.

I am always worried about the way body positioning is over-emphasized in karate. If I am expecting an attack and get myself into the proper position for it, then all well and good; but if I am surprised whilst sitting down, how do I employ those positions?

When I began karate, I used to punch by driving my fist forward like an express train. Much later I discovered that it is much better to throw your fist at the target, keeping forearm and wrist rather (but not completely) relaxed. As the punch contacts, I tighten my fist and forearm as much as I can and provided the spasm is strong enough, the weapon has all the mass of a sledgehammer, penetrating deep into the target.

The trick is to restrict the tightened muscles to those of the forearm because if you bring in the shoulders and body, the punch slows when it should be accelerating. The way I train to localise the contraction is to squeeze my fist as tightly as possible whilst bending and straightening my forearm in rapid movements.

What led me into this discovery was listening to a Japanese karate instructor friend describing to me how the most powerful punch he had ever taken was delivered in a relaxed, almost casual manner by Master Ohtsuka, the founder of wado ryu. By that time, Master Ohtsuka was well into his seventies. It is clear that he could not have used the more obvious and physically demanding principles commonly used by karateka and I have never forgotten this example.

So whether you kick, punch, or strike, start off relaxed and throw the weapon into the target, only tightening up as you are about to land and then localising the contraction in the weapon area itself.

Returning to more mundane theory, let us review the way in which body positioning can enhance the force of a punch. Regardless of the technique you intend to employ, try and move your body weight behind it. A shift of body weight forwards over a couple of inches, although not a great distance, is sufficient to produce a force called 'momentum'. Momentum is a powerful force possessed by moving bodies and if harnessed to the punch, will give a substantial bonus in impact energy.

This energy is also invaluable in soaking up the recoil produced by a blow and this is particularly important if you are a small person striking a larger opponent. Correct usage of momentum allows you to reduce energy loss through recoil even when punching whilst standing on one leg! If you do not generate momentum during your punch, lock your rear knee joint so the leg is straight and can act like a prop.

Try and develop power from the hips. The pelvic girdle is situated near the body's centre of gravity and techniques delivered through it lose little from the flexing of the body. This is well known to goju ryu karateka and it is the reason for a prolonged study of the kata sanchin. Recoil produced by a powerful punch delivered directly from shoulder height drives the upper body back and squanders energy.

A friend of mine who practises goju ryu made up a training rig to develop power from the centre of gravity. It uses one of those pull-weights you see attached to gymnasium walls. You stand with your back to the wall and push the handle forwards and away from you. As you do, a wire rope passes over a pulley and lifts a weight. On George's modified rig, the power take-off is lowered to waist height.

When I first tried it, I could only lift the weight by leaning forward, showing that I was unable to develop adequate power through my centre of gravity. Only after a lot of practice and correct usage of stance can the weight be lifted. This is an excellent way of developing real power in your techniques.

To return to the description, if you turn your hips behind a technique, you harness a part of this power and at the same time, your spine is slightly twisted. By letting the hip twist first, the spine is tensioned and when released, it sweeps the upper body around with it, driving the shoulder forward behind the blow.

Moving both arms together accelerates the shoulders behind a punch. It is vital that on impact, the fist is still accelerating, though as near to maximum speed as possible – so make sure your range is accurate and this can best be achieved by practising with the impact pad.

A final component is rotation of the forearm from a palm-upwards to palm-downwards position on impact. This is said to add further power to a punch but I have always found it difficult to master when using a makiwara or impact pad. Nevertheless it is standard karate practice, so drive the fist forcefully round whilst keeping your wrist rigid (so it doesn't fold on impact).

Shukokai stylists only rotate their fists part-way when attacking high targets. They reason logically that when punching upwards with the palm rotated fully downwards, the lower knuckle joints contact first, causing pain and laceration.

Whether delivering a punch, kick or strike, it always makes sense to withdraw the hand or foot promptly afterwards, so it cannot be avoided and caught by the opponent.

Kicks are naturally more powerful because the leg has a substantial mass. Nevertheless they can be improved by putting body weight behind them through a slight forward movement of the body during delivery. Twisting the hips into the kick also adds power.

If you have coordinated your kick correctly, impact is made just as the hips complete their swivel (or push) forwards. Acceleration into the target comes primarily from the upper leg and maximum limb speed should be approaching as the knee reaches correct height.

Kiai

Watching Wimbledon in the summer, I noticed a few players making loud grunting noises as they slammed the ball. This happened as they tensed their diaphragms to inject every last ounce of power. In karate this happens too and is called *kiai*. The meaning is rather difficult to translate but indicates a harmony of resolve between the will to act and the body.

At the conclusion of a powerful technique or block, the karateka injects every ounce of power and determination, locking up all the muscles for an instant of time. As the diaphragm (the muscular band below the ribs and responsible for breathing) tightens, air is driven out and gives rise to the kiai.

The sound it makes is formed into a short, explosive, monosyllabic 'EEE!', though some people add a descending (and unnecessary) tail-off to it. The sound is deep pitched and quite unlike the shriek produced if the air comes from the upper chest, forced out by the action of the intercostal muscles instead of the diaphragm (*fig 68*).

Figure 68

Reaction speed, co-ordination, minimum effective distance and timing all play a part in the correct response to an attack.

Kiai is used at specified points during the performance of katas and usually when turning to face a new direction.

Various claims are made for the power produced by it but I remain sceptical and wonder if any power produced is as a result of muscular tension rather than the shout itself. I must also question the commitment of all the body's energies into a technique which may miss and then take time to recover.

One thing is certain – that when the body is tightened by the spasm of kiai, it becomes able to absorb a great deal of impact energy. This is very useful as long as you can arrange to kiai every time you are hit.

Certain schools make a habit of kiai on every punch or block. Not only is this very wearing on the throat and eardrums, but I am not sure whether each kiai truly does represent a total commitment to a technique. What it undoubtedly does do though, is raise the martial spirit amongst the class so perhaps that is its raison d'être.

ON THE RIGHT FOOT

Karate places great emphasis on taking up the correct stance. Some stances are purely formal, such as the attention stance you adopt after the kneeling bow (*fig 69*). Others are meant to facilitate a certain course of action and may be held only for a few instants before being changed.

Stance is a fluid thing, constantly adapting to suit a changing situation. Learn how to move freely by first learning each stance, then how to change one into the other. Always be in the right stance, at the right distance, at the right time.

Figure 69

Figure 70   Figure 71

Let's talk about the guard next. I love the kung fu films that
show people standing in the most unlikely stances, with arms
raised high and fingers pointing. These look very menacing but
from the point of view of efficiency, they are a dead loss. The
object of guard is to place your hands and body so it is difficult
for your opponent to hit you while your options remain open.

Your arms must be carried so that either one can be used
quickly. Your feet must be angled so you can make a correct evasion, advance, or retreat. Your body must be turned so as to
make a small target for your opponent whilst leaving your arms
and legs in the correct attitude for instant use.

In general terms, this means turning your body slightly away
from the opponent by withdrawing the hip on that side. The
front foot turns slightly inwards to close your groin. If your left
foot leads, then your left hand does too. If you lead from left
stance with your right hand, a large area of your body will be
exposed to attack (*fig 70*), so this is an unwise posture to adopt
unless you are performing a specific technique requiring this
change of guard.

Your non-leading hand must be held closer to the body, where
it can either catch attacks which get past the front hand, or
deliver a powerful punch or strike. Close off the front of your
body by bringing both arms into the midline of your body (*fig
71*).

Figure 72   Figure 73

The ready stance

We've already discussed attention stance. Starting from it, step out a half-pace with your left foot, followed by a half-pace with the right. At the same time clench your fists. If your stance is correct, the outer edges of your feet should be vertically below your shoulders (*fig 72*). This is called 'ready stance', or *shizentai* and it represents an awareness of the imminence of action.

If you step forward a half-pace from ready stance with left or right foot, you adopt a useful variety of ready stance. The body remains upright and the hands are held at the sides. Weight distribution is even over both legs and the leading foot points forwards (*fig 73*).

Cat stance

From ready stance, bring your weight over the rear foot and bend the knee. Extend your leading leg slightly and raise the heel from the floor. Hardly any weight rests on the ball of the front foot. This is called 'cat stance', or *neko ashi* (*fig 74*).

Common mistakes are putting too much weight on the front foot, turning the front foot in– or outwards, body lean, or pushing your bottom out.

Back stance

Extend your forward foot and let the heel drop but not touch the floor. Let your back foot rotate outwards, so an angle of ninety degrees or more opens between the two feet. The feet should lie in one straight line. Keep your weight over the back foot (*fig 75*). Note that hips have now turned sideways on and though more weight presses on the front foot, by far the greater weight remains on the rear.

This stance is called 'back stance', or *kokutso dachi*. It suffers from the same faults as does cat stance.

Figure 74

Figure 75

Figure 76

Fighting stance

From back stance, move your weight forward so there is a 50/50 distribution over both feet. Slide your front foot to the side to produce what is called 'sidestep'. This is necessary to give you side-to-side balance. Turn your front foot slightly inwards and rotate the back foot so it faces towards the front. Bend both knees equally. This stance is used a lot during sparring and is therefore called 'fighting stance', or *hanmei gamae* (*fig 76*).

The stance mustn't be so long as to make forwards and backwards movement too laboured; neither must it be too short, allowing you to be run back off balance by a determined attacker.

Forward stance

From fighting stance, advance your weight so your front knee comes to lie immediately above the instep. Turn the leading foot so it points straight ahead. If the stance is to be stable in a forwards and backwards direction, your shin must rise vertically to the knee and not angle to either side. Turn your hips completely to the front and straighten your rear leg, locking the knee so it can function like a prop. The rear foot is turned forwards and the heel is settled firmly on the floor (*fig 77*). This stance is particularly strong for punches and blocks.

There are several faults to avoid in 'forward stance', or *zenkutsu dachi* as it is known. The height varies from style to style but the width is always such that the outer edges of the feet are vertically below the shoulders. Too much sidestep and your groin is open to attack; too little and the stance is unstable. If the front knee is not bent enough, the foot is light and stability is lost. If the leading knee falls inwards, the stance is weakened. If the rear heel is off the floor or the knee is bent, the stance's ability to absorb recoil is reduced.

Reverse punch stance

Draw the front foot back and outwards, whilst rotating it slightly inwards. Twist the hips even more to the front and the result is called 'reverse punch stance' (*fig 78*). Push outwards on the leading knee to prevent it sagging inwards.

Figure 77 *Figure 78*

Hourglass stance

If you pull your front foot back from reverse punch stance so the heel is in line with the toes of the rear foot, then the result is *sanchin*, or 'hourglass stance'. (*fig 79*). The hips must be raised and projected forwards so the groin is protected from upswinging kicks and the stance is strengthened.

Straddle stance

Two forms of straddle stances appear in karate. Both resemble the position taken by someone on horseback. The height of stance varies from style to style but the configuration is the same with the body upright and weight evenly distributed.

Step to the side from ready stance, first with the left foot, then with the right. Let your feet rotate outwards slightly but make sure your knees are directly above your ankles (*fig 80*). This version is called *shikodachi*.

Figure 79

Figure 80

Figure 81

In the second and more difficult form, rotate your feet so they converge slightly. This puts a tremendous strain on the knees and calves and is called *kibadachi* (*fig 81*). A common fault is to drop the knees inwards instead of forcing them out and this leads to a weak stance. Keep your back straight and don't let your backside poke out.

BASIC TECHNIQUES

The basic techniques of karate are the fundamental punches and kicks practised in a formal manner. The class will usually perform them in lines, advancing until space is used up, then turning on command to advance in the reverse direction. The first basic technique you will encounter is 'lunge punch'.

Lunge punch

Lunge punch is known either as *oi zuki*, or *junzuki*. It is practised from forward stance and the height of delivery is varied

Figure 82   *Figure 83*

according to the instructions given. *Jodan* punches are aimed towards the face, *chudan* towards the midsection and *gedan* towards the lower stomach and groin.

Start from right forward stance and extend your right arm forward, closing the fist and turning the knuckles upwards. The fist is brought across the chest to the midline. The left fist is held at belt height with the palm rotated upward (*fig 82*). Step forwards into left stance, holding your right arm steady as you do so (*fig 83*). As the new stance takes shape (*fig 84*), pull back your right arm and at the same time, punch with your left. Rotate both fists simultaneously at the end of travel (*fig 85*).

Getting the step correct is quite difficult and novices usually find their stance widening or narrowing as they progress. Whilst concentrating on the step, they sometimes forget to keep their knees bent and so bob up and down.

Timing of the punch is critical. It must land on target whilst the body is still moving, to gain from the momentum generated; but if started too early, it pulls the step off balance.

Figure 84

Figure 85

Reverse punch

Practise reverse punch from forward stance by first punching without stepping forward (*figs 86 & 87*). This ensures that your correct arm is leading. As you punch, turn your hips so that the stance is both shortened and widened.

When stepping forward to reverse punch, turn the front foot outwards, then transfer weight in the usual manner but as you bring your rear foot forward, also curve it inward so it glides past the front leg (*fig 88*). Then allow it to curve out by the same distance and deflection. As you complete the step, rotate both feet so they are parallel or slightly converging.

Hold your leading arm well forward and don't wave it about or swing your shoulders as you step.

As you take up the new stance, pull back your leading arm and begin to move your rear shoulder, lifting the rear fist away from your hip. As your withdrawing arm accelerates, so does the punch and they pass each other in front of the chest (*fig 89*).

As weight finally settles on the front foot, firmly clench your fists and simultaneously tighten and rotate both through one hundred and eighty degrees (*fig 90*).

Figure 86   Figure 87

Figure 88

Figure 89

Figure 90

Figure 91   *Figure 92*

Front kick

Practise front kick from fighting stance (*fig 91*) by first changing your guard and twisting your supporting leg. As this happens (i.e., not after it), raise your right leg, lifting the sole directly off the floor (*fig 92*). Don't lift the heel first or you will find it difficult to get your foot into the correct configuration. Bring your knee up until it is pointing at the target in one smooth, accelerating line (*fig 93*). Keep your elbows to your side so they don't flap about.

As your knee is reaching correct height, begin driving your lower leg out, so the sole of your foot travels horizontally into the target, with toes pulled back (*fig 94*). After delivering the kick, pull your foot back and set it down gently.

Roundhouse kick

From left fighting stance, strongly rotate your shoulders to the left and lift the right foot off the floor (*fig 95*). Its path is distorted by the right hip, which swivels through greater than ninety degrees of angle (*fig 96*). This can be seen as rotation of the supporting leg.

Figure 93

Figure 94

Figure 95

Figure 96

Figure 97   *Figure 98*

Lean away from the rising kick because if you don't, you will inhibit hip action and make your kick unstable. As the knee rotates to face the target, begin straightening your lower leg with toes either pointed or pulled back (*fig 97*). If you rotate your hips sufficiently, your right hip will rise until it is directly above the left and you turn fully sideways as the foot slams home (*fig 98*).

Side kick

Side kick is best demonstrated from a straddle stance, holding your fists in a guard position. Slide forwards with your rear leg (*fig 99*) and as you do, lift your leading foot straight off the floor rapidly bringing it to the correct height (*fig 100*). Without pause, drive it directly and heel-first into the target (*figs 101 & 102*). Remember to lift your big toe and depress the others (*fig 103*). Lean back to counterbalance the weight of your extending leg. After kicking, pull your whole leg back against your chest before setting it down.

Figure 99

Figure 100

Figure 101

Figure 102

Figure 103

Figure 104

Figure 105

Figure 106

Figure 107

Figure 108

Back kick

Practise back kick from a fighting stance which has little side-step (*fig 104*). Rotate your body and drive your front leg up and back in a straight line to the target (*figs 105 & 106*). Strike with the heel, pointing the toes towards the floor (*fig 107*).

Turn your hips fully or the kick will be off centre. Pull the kicking leg back to your chest and twist your hips back forwards before you set your foot down (*fig 108*).

COMBINATION TECHNIQUES

Basic techniques can be linked together into a series, such that after the first, the next in line is already teed up and ready to go. Whereas one technique can be blocked, a whole series coming at different targets from differing angles puts the defender under pressure and one may slip in. The most elementary combination technique is the block and punch, where the former deflects an attack, providing an opening for the punch which follows it.

When assembling techniques, choose those which follow each other naturally. Then select a different target for each technique, so the defender has to use a variety of blocks to cope. Make the techniques follow each other as quickly as possible and be able to do them whilst advancing, retreating, or evading.

Maintain balance and guard throughout the combination. Make sure each technique is performed properly before the next is used. There is a tendency for people to gloss over the first techniques, concentrating all their efforts on the last. This is bad practice. Withdraw each technique properly after use.

At first, the instructor will select the combinations you need to practise. These will start off simple, with two or three techniques. As you become more proficient, so additional and more difficult techniques will be added. Eventually, you will be in a position to make up your own combination techniques, practising them in front of a mirror, so you can see any mistakes or openings.

The following are some examples of combination techniques but do experiment and discover those which suit you best.

Start in left fighting stance and front kick with your right leg (*fig 109*). Change guard first, keeping your elbows close to your sides and shoulders relaxed. Set your kicking leg down in front, ball of foot first and as weight descends, draw back your right arm, twist the hips forward and reverse punch strongly with your left arm (*figs 110 & 111*), withdrawing it afterwards.

Figure 109   Figure 110

Figure 111

Figure 112   *Figure 113*

The second sequence is slightly more complicated. Start as before in left fighting stance and step quickly forwards into right fighting stance, snap punching to the face with your right fist as you come to a stop (*fig 112*). Follow this with strong pull-back and a left reverse punch to midsection (*fig 113*). As you pull back the punch, bring your left hip around (*fig 114*) and deliver a left roundhouse kick to the head (*fig 115*).

Figure 114   *Figure 115*

EVASION TECHNIQUES

Evasion techniques take the body away from an attack. Usually they are accompanied by a block or guard. The simplest evasion is a step backwards and if you don't retreat too far, you can deliver an immediate counter-attack. Where a full step is not indicated, pull your body back over the rear leg and shorten your stance (*figs 116 & 117*).

Sideways evasion is another option but make sure it takes you away from the attack, not into it. For the first technique, take up left fighting stance (*fig 118*) and step to the outside with your left leg, maintaining an effective guard (*fig 119*). Continue by swivelling your hips in a clockwise direction (*fig 120*).

Figure 116

Figure 117

Figure 118   Figure 119   Figure 120

Figure 121   *Figure 122*

Because you stepped to the side and swivelled your hips, you removed your body from the line of attack and the block served only as a guard. A small sidestep leaves you close enough to an opponent to follow with a punch.

The second evasion technique works well when you are in opposite stance to the opponent. This time step diagonally outwards and back with your rear foot (*figs 121 & 122*). This pulls you back and out of line. Draw up your left leg (*fig 123*) and turn your hips fully away, leaning forwards and blocking outwards with your left forearm (*fig 124*).

The next technique is not strictly an evasion. It is actually a 'jamming' technique – one which prevents an attack from being properly delivered. However, it is convenient to examine it here.

Both of you begin from left stance and as your partner attempts to kick you, spring forwards using the power in your bent back leg. Close distance and block downwards with your left forearm against his knee, catching it before it reaches the necessary height. Because you moved onto the technique, it has insufficient time to develop power and can be jammed without injury to yourself.

Keep your groin closed and as you block, punch to his chest with your right fist (*fig 125*).

Figure 123

Figure 124

Figure 125

BLOCKS

A block is a technique which diverts an attack so it misses its target. Skilled karateka use the minimum of force in a block to obtain the greatest deflection of the attacking limb. They achieve this by blocking at an angle to the attack, so the latter is redirected away. By this means, a skilled small person can deflect the attacks of a larger opponent.

Stronger karateka sometimes use blocks as a means of attack, smashing the opponent's forearm or shin with a powerful, clubbing block. This requires sturdy arms and/or correct timing and distancing.

Typical blocks use the forearm or edge of the hand to deflect an attack.

Knife block

Knife block uses the cutting action of knifehand to deflect a punch or strike. Take up left back stance and extend your left arm out from the body, turning it palm downwards and bending the elbow. Bring your right hand across your chest and turn it

Figure 126

palm upwards (*fig 126*). Don't bend your wrists and keep the thumbs firmly locked into palms.

Step forwards into right back stance and as you do so, straighten your left arm completely whilst bringing the right palm up to cup your left ear (*fig 127*). As your hips rotate into the new stance, strongly pull back your left arm and rotate the forearm so the palm turns upwards. Cut outwards and across with the right, twisting your forearm at the last moment, so the palm rotates forwards (*fig 128*).

This block is powered by the rotation of your hips and by the pull-back of the leading hand.

Figure 127

Figure 128

Figure 129   *Figure 130*   *Figure 131*

Midsection outer block

This uses a sweeping movement of the forearm to deflect attacks to the chest. Start in left forward stance with your left arm bent by ninety degrees at the elbow. Your knuckles face forwards and are held at shoulder height. Your right fist sits palm upwards on the right hip (*fig 129*).

Step into right forwards stance and as you do so, straighten your left arm and extend the fingers, turning the hand palm downwards. Bring your right arm across your chest with the thumb pressing into your ribs (*fig 130*). As you finish stepping forwards, withdraw your left arm as strongly as possible, rotating it palm upwards as it comes to rest on the left hip. Use this action to power your right arm as it travels out and across your chest, coming to a stop with strong forearm rotation in front of your right shoulder (*fig 131*). Block with the thumb side of your forearm. It is not necessary to block past the line of your shoulder.

Figure 132   *Figure 133*   *Figure 134*

Midsection inner block

Start off as above in left forward stance but bring your left arm further across your body (*fig 132*). As you step, extend and open your left arm and bring your right off the hip and into a saluting position near your right ear (*fig 133*). As the step concludes, draw back your left arm, closing and rotating the fist. Swing your right arm down and across your body, rotating it knuckles-forward as it reaches the midline (*fig 134*). Block with the little finger side of your forearm.

   Don't let your fist get in front as you block and check that the action does not knock the attack down into your stomach.

Lower block

Lower block also uses the little finger side of your forearm to deflect an attack aimed at the stomach. Start in left forward stance and extend your left arm downwards, so the fist is held

| *Figure 135* | *Figure 136* | *Figure 137* |

above and slightly to the side of the front knee. Keep your right fist on your hip (*fig 135*).

Step into right forward stance and as you do, bring your right arm up and across your body, so the fist rests with the little finger against your left shoulder (*fig 136*). As you stop moving forwards, pull back and rotate your left arm, so the fist finishes palm upwards against the left hip. At the same time, drive your right arm down and away from your body, locking the elbow straight and rotating the forearm (*fig 137*). Don't block past your knee.

Upper block

Upper block uses a complicated rolling action of the forearm as it moves diagonally upwards and forwards. This makes it equally effective against both descending and straight blows to the face and head.

Begin from left forward stance with right fist on your hip. Your left arm is raised so the forearm leans upwards and out from the body. The knuckles are turned back towards the face (*fig 138*). The forearm must slope upwards from elbow to wrist so any descending techniques will be deflected off it. The arm must reach well forwards to meet attacks early on.

Figure 138

Figure 139

Figure 140

Figure 141

Step into right forward stance and as you do, straighten your left arm and extend the fingers (*fig 139*). Pull your left arm back onto the hip and drive your right up and forwards (*fig 140*), leaving it until the last minute to rotate the forearm (*fig 141*).

PRE-ARRANGED SPARRING

Semi-free sparring follows on naturally from combination technique, allowing karate techniques to be tried out on an opponent in controlled circumstances. No amount of training against pads or bags can equip you for combat with another person so semi-free sparring is the ideal introduction.

Consider the following sequence. The defender stands in ready stance and the attacker faces him in left fighting stance (*fig 142*). The attacker steps forward into right stance and punches to the defender's face but the latter has stepped back with his left leg and deflects the attack with upper block (*fig 143*). Pausing for an instant the attacker then steps forward into left forward stance and punches a second time. The defender moves back simultaneously into right forward stance and again uses upwards block (*fig 144*). The attacker steps forwards and punches a third time and the defender steps back, blocks as before, then pulls back his block and reverse-punches to the attacker's ribs (*fig 145*).

This is a very simple form of three-step prearranged sparring and illustrates a number of characteristics of this form of practice. Firstly the attack and defence are agreed beforehand between both parties. Secondly there are three consecutive attacks and defences. Thirdly, the sequence concludes with the delivery of an effective technique.

Three step sparring teaches you distancing, timing and focus. You begin by taking up the correct distance apart as defined by the attacker. The latter must be able to reach the target comfortably with the selected attack. During each advance and step back, this distance must be maintained by varying the length of the stance. Timing is important and if you defend too slowly, the attack will overtake you. You must move immediately the attacker does. Maintain coordination throughout, to ensure you have the correct arm and leg leading and focus the concluding technique effectively on the target.

Figure 142

Figure 143

Figure 144

Figure 145

In the second basic sequence, the attacker has chosen to use three front kicks. He starts in left stance and kicks with his right foot (*fig 146*). The defender quickly steps back into left fighting stance, withdrawing his body out of the kick's range. After the briefest of pauses, the attacker kicks with his left leg and the defender steps back with his left foot (*fig 147*). On the third attack, the defender evades the kick by stepping back and to the side with his right foot, swivelling his hips in the same direction. At the same time, he sweeps the kick to the side, catching it with his forearm (*fig 148*). To avoid injury, the blocking arm must be closed into a fist.

The block lifts and displaces the kick, allowing a strong right reverse punch to be delivered to the attacker's head (*fig 149*). Don't wait too long after he lands to punch.

One-step sparring is a lot faster and in the example I have chosen, the opponents face each other in left fighting stances. The attacker lifts his right knee up to perform a roundhouse kick but before he can do so, the defender drives forward off his back leg and thrusts his left knife hand into the attacker's chest, unbalancing him (*fig 150*).

Figure 146

Figure 147

Figure 148

Figure 149

Figure 150

Always remain within striking distance after you evade your opponent's attack.

Timing is very important because the attacker must be caught on one leg and before the kick has developed. If you counter too slowly, you will probably collect a resounding whack from the shin of the kicking leg. Distance is also important and if you are too far away, you will not be able to close in time.

It is possible to make up prearranged sparring sequences to test blocks, evasions and counter attacks but always make sure your partner knows exactly what is required and what will happen.

A more advanced form of prearranged sparring designates the attack but leaves the response free. The attacker may be restricted to using only roundhouse kick but he can change legs, kick high or low, with or without a step. The defender can use any technique in response to that attack.

Once you are proficient in dealing with this form of training, you are ready for free sparring.

SPARRING AND COMPETITION

The beginner will not encounter either free sparring or competition in a well-run club because both involve combat during which blows and kicks of quite considerable force may be exchanged. Before you can spar, you must therefore understand the basic principles of evasion, distance, timing and blocking. Until you have a working knowledge of these and in addition, can punch and kick without injuring yourself, it is foolish to attempt sparring.

Not all students like sparring, yet it is a necessary part of training. I have known many students who were either frightened, or felt completely useless at it. Those who were frightened I encouraged by putting them with sensible high grades who could be relied upon to avoid excesses. Unfortunately some senior karateka have an ego problem which causes them to knock lower grades about as a means of reinforcing their status. Such people are not good karateka. Some students feel inadequate because their partner is obviously much better than they are. These can be encouraged by always partnering them with people who will spar at their own pace.

Having said all that, if the student has no will to improve, then no coaching method on earth will be successful.

Sparring in the class usually takes place at the end of the training session. You may either select a partner, or the club instructor will select one for you. When selecting your own partner, find one of equal size and either the same, or higher grade. Lower grades are less experienced at sparring and have little control over their techniques. Beginner karateka should not be allowed to spar together for this reason.

Large people develop a lot of power, even when attacking slowly and smaller opponents should be careful not to pit their strength directly against superior force.

You may not attack the opponent's shin, ankle, knee, or groin. When I began training, both the shin and the groin were legitimate targets but these have now been eliminated to encourage people to try for more advanced techniques.

Close your hands fully when attacking the face and control your impact so no injury is caused. Many facial injuries are caused when the opponent runs onto or ducks into a technique. Use control also when attacking body targets, though because these are less prone to injury, you may land with a greater degree of force. When fighting a lighter opponent, take extra care not to cause injury with the force of your techniques.

The object of free sparring is not to clobber your opponent but to engage him/her in a battle of technique. It is sufficient merely to touch the opponent with your technique to indicate its success. If you are lightly tapped with a successful technique, withdraw for an instant before resuming. This signifies to the opponent that you recognise that attack as valid. This courtesy prevents sparring from degenerating into a brawl. The only

The karate technique develops tremendous power, and impact must be carefully controlled.

alternative is to sink techniques in with full force and this is not something I would recommend.

Sometimes the instructor will make you spar at reduced speed. This is a valuable exercise for teaching you how to react under pressure. It is far from easy and frequent practice leads to efficient use of blocks, evasions, timing and combination techniques.

If ever sparring gets out of hand, and/or your opponent seems to be getting over-excited, withdraw and bow. Then go and sit down cross-legged at the side of the dojo.

Competition is a form of free sparring in which half– or full point scores are awarded for successful techniques delivered to scoring areas of the head, face and body. A maximum of three points may be scored by one opponent in a two, or three minute bout. The scoring areas include the head, face and the body (excluding the groin and tips of the shoulders). No contact to the

The hips play a major role in the development of power and effective range.

throat or groin is allowed and no open-hand technique can be made to the face.

To score, the technique must have all the attributes of good form and land in a controlled manner on the scoring area. Any infringement of the rules is dealt with by either a warning, a half point penalty, a full point penalty, or loss by a foul. In extreme cases, the offender can be disqualified from further participation in the tournament.

The match is scored by a referee and judge who remain on opposite sides of the competitors. An arbitrator sits at the edge of the match area to ensure that the rules are correctly followed by all parties. The match area itself is an eight metre matted square. Under no circumstances should you compete on a solid floor.

Matches are fought in both team and individual categories. Mens' teams consist of five men plus two reserves. Womens' teams comprise three women plus one reserve. In the mens' individual division, there is a junior category for under twenty-one year olds. Womens' individual competition is held in three weight divisions, mens' competition in seven.

Tournaments also include team and individual kata competitions. These are typically three-round affairs with the first round eliminating down to sixteen and the second round down to eight. The winner and runners-up are selected from the last eight in the third round.

KATA

Kata is an advanced form of training that used to be the highest expression of karate before the advent of free sparring. The word *kata* does not translate readily and the approximation most often encountered is 'pattern', or 'form'.

Over seventy katas are practised nowadays, each consisting of a whole series of techniques arranged in a set order and direction. Some katas are purely training forms, others teach principles of strength, speed or balance. They are also excellent training systems, teaching how to link techniques in a viable sequence whilst building physical endurance.

Most katas are symmetrical, starting from and finishing on the same spot. This is used by the instructor to check the uniformity of your performance.

Some karate training involves the pitting of antagonistic muscles against each other to develop strength.

You will encounter katas at an early stage in your training. The first you will learn are called *pinans*, or *heians* as they are called in the shotokan school. The pinans were developed at the turn of the century as part of a special syllabus taught in schools. There are five pinans and one must be learned for each of the elementary grades. These are followed by a whole series of more advanced katas, the number varying according to the style practised. Goju ryu has the least number of katas in its syllabus and shito ryu the most.

Start from ready stance, then bow and move into attention stance, clenching your fists. At first the kata is practised in single steps, each at the instructor's command. At the conclusion, the instructor will call "*Yamei*" and you withdraw from the last position into ready stance. At conclusion of the lesson's kata practice, draw your heels together and perform a standing bow.

Once you have learned the moves, the instructor will have you perform them in sequences. Each sequence consists of a series of techniques separated by pauses and represents a response to an imaginary sparring situation. During the pause, the next threat is being assessed.

When you perform sequences at full speed, try not to blur techniques together. Each has a definite start and end. When you pause, allow a count of at least two seconds and always turn your head to look before turning in a new direction.

Once you have learned all the techniques and the sequences in which they occur, you will be allowed to perform the kata all the way through. Remember that it is not a race to finish in the shortest possible time and at the conclusion, remain in your last stance until called back to ready stance by the instructor.

At certain points in the kata, all the body's energies will be focussed towards a block or punch. When this happens, make a strong kiai. During the performance of kata, aim for fluidity and balance and avoid unnecessary hesitations in performance. Breathe properly and concentrate your attention in the correct direction.

You can never practise enough kata. At first you must spend all your time trying to remember which move follows which. After many hours of practice, the moves become automatic and your mind becomes free to dwell on the meaning of the kata itself. You can then concentrate on putting a polish on each move.

Some instructors try to explain in practical terms, the meaning of the moves in kata. This is quite difficult to do since many

Great deliberation is used during the execution of techniques.

katas involved the usage of covert weapons and without them, some techniques now have no obvious meaning. In other cases, no true application can be traced – though if one were to search far enough back into karate's history, one might find it. Despite this, personal interpretations can and are placed upon the various moves and through this, the student can see a purpose in what is being practised.

Acknowledgements

Many people have contributed either directly or indirectly to this book. My career in karate, short though it is thus far, has been illuminated by the opinions and teachings of and cooperation and discussions with the following:

Len Palmer, who introduced me to karate and apart from that one small mistake, did more than anyone else to establish karate in Britain back in those early days.

Tatsuo Suzuki, 8th Dan, who was my first teacher and established my interest in karate.

Toru Takamizawa 6th Dan, who was my second teacher and the latter-day author of two fascinating works on karate that caused me to re-think my approach to what I had been doing for more than twenty years.

Peter Spanton 6th Dan who was my third teacher and friend. It was my good luck to train under one of Britain's finest black belts.

Mitsusuke Harada who, over many years, has given me the benefit of his recollections of early karate development in Japan.

Yasunari Ishimi 7th Dan, who attempted the impossible in explaining to me the meaning of 'The Way of Karate'.

David 'Ticky' Donovan 7th Dan, the British National Coach, for his in-depth analysis of competition karate technique.

Keiji Tomiyama 6th Dan, who has made a study of the development of karate and who kindly explained the lineage of the various *ryu* in Japan and Okinawa.

Tommy Morris 6th Dan, who has developed the theory of high-impact karate to the level of a science.

Bernard Creton 5th Dan for making known his studies on stance and power development.

George Andrews 4th Dan for demonstrating the correct usage of the makiwara and the body's centre of gravity.

Rex Hazeldine of the National Coaching Foundation for his fascinating lectures on fitness

Doctor James Canney, the Chief Medical Officer of the Martial Arts Commission, for his advice on safety.

And last but not least, Peter Stanton and Clive East for assisting with the photographs used in this book.

Useful addresses

Amateur Karate Kai
Style: Wado ryu
Distribution: Midlands
Mr J McCann 47 Patrick Road
Corley
Northants

Amateur Martial Arts Association
Style: Wado ryu & Shotokan
Distribution: National
Mrs N Powell
10 Coppice Close
Stratford on Avon
Warwickshire CU37 6TN

Amateur Shotokan Karate Association
Style: Shotokan
Distribution: National
Mr D Martin
84 Ounsdale Road
Wombourne
Wolverhampton
West Midlands WV5 8BW

Mr D Bradley
5 Brackendale Close
Hounslow
Middlesex TW3 4AZ

Association of Nippon Kempo
Style: Nippon kempo
Distribution: London, Liverpool
Mr L De Gale
1 Halford Road
Fulham
London SW6

British American Karate Clubs
Style: Mugendo
Distribution: London
Mr B S Johal
32 Palmerston Road
Forest Gate
London E7

British Isles Karate Association
Style: Wado ryu
Distribution: Lancs, N. Yorkshire and Tyne & Wear
Mr G Watkins
7 Bleasby Street
Sneiton Dale
Sneiton
Nottingham

British Karate Association
Style: Free style
Distribution: Manchester & North
Mr D Connor
Oriental World
18 Swan Street
Manchester

British Karate Ishinryu
Style: Ishin ryu
Distribution: Greater London, Essex
Mr D Donovan
133–135 High Street South
East Ham

British Karate-Do Chojinkai
Style: Wado ryu
Distribution: Cumbria, Cleveland, Tyne & Wear W Midlands
Mr D A James
'Greenacres'
High Hesket
Carlisle
Cumbria CA4 0HU

British Karate-Jutsu Karate-Do Kai
Style: Karate-Jutsu
Distribution: National
Mr B Creton,
54, Albert Road,
Folkestone,
Kent

Mr E Spencer-Brown,
2nd Floor,
26, Lower Stone Street,
Maidstone,
Kent
Tel: 0622 688167

British Okinawan Karate Bugeikai
Style: Okinawan Karate
Distribution: Hampshire, Sussex
Mr R Woodhams
Greenways
Mill Lane
Titchfield
PO15 5DU

British Sankukai Karate Association
Style: Sankukai
Distribution: Worcs & Beds
Mr K Beddoe
8 Perrin Avenue
Kidderminster
DV11 6LL

British Shito-Ryu Kenshinkan
Style: Shito ryu
Distribution: South of England
Mr R Mills,
14, Beech Glen,
Crowthorne Road,
Bracknell,
Berks RG12 4DQ.
Tel: 0344 55339

British Shotokan Karate Shinboku Association
Style: Shotokan
Distribution: National
Mr C Mack
28 Ashburnham Mansions
Ashburnham Road
London SW10

Bukonkai Karate International
Style: Shotokan
Distribution: National
Mr C Williams
49 Kingsway
Newton
Chester

Codrington European Karate Development Organisation
Style: Wado ryu
Distribution: West Midlands, London
Mr E Codrington
18, Handsworth Wood Road,
Handsworth Wood,
Birmingham,
B20 2DS.

Elite Karate Association
Style: Wado ryu
Distribution: West Midlands
Mr J Johnson,
56, Chetwynd Road
Penn,
Wolverhampton
Tel: 0902 334666

English Contact Karate Association
Style: Semi-Contact
Distribution: National
Mr M Haig,
BA1 Building,
99, John Bright Street
Birmingham B1 1B
Tel: 021 643 4270

English Goju-Ryu Karate-Do Association
Style: Goju ryu
Distribution: National
Mr G Malone
5 Elfindale Road
Herne Hill
London SE24
Tel: 01 274 6376

English Karate Organisation
Style: Multi-style
Distribution: National
Mr R Evans
124 Warwick Street
Leamington Spa
Warks CV32 4QY

England Karatedo Wadokai
Style: Wado ryu
Distribution: Teeside, Coventry
Mr W Seaton
111 Norton Road
Stockton on Tees
Cleveland

English Korean Karate Association
Style: Korean Karate
Distribution: Suffolk
Mr J Day
3 Fen Farm Cottages
Washbrook
Ipswich
Suffolk IP8 3HE

English Shotokan Karate Association
Style: Shotokan
Distribution: North London, Beds Essex, Herts
Mr R Hall
Flat 5 Elsenham Hall
Elsenham
Bishops Stortford
Herts

Great Britain Karate Federation
Style: Wado ryu & Shotokan
Distribution: National
Mrs I Haywood
12 Newhorse Road
Cheslyn Hay
Walsall
Staffs

Higashi Karate Kai
Style: Wado ryu
Distribution: National
Mr P Whitney
17 Martinsfield
Covingham
Swindon
Wiltshire

International Karate Union
Style: Multi-style
Distribution: West Midlands London
Mr T Steward,
29, Beaminster Gardens
Barkingside,
Essex
Tel: 01 550 1222

International Sankukai Karate Association
Style: Sankukai
Distribution: Home Counties
Mr B Stranack
12 Monkton Close
Ferndown
Wimborne
BH22 9LL

In Yo Kan Karate Association
Style: Wado ryu
Distribution: London & South East
Ms A Shortell
3 Hamilton Road
Southall
Middlesex
UB1 3BQ

Jin Sei Kai Karate Association
Style: Shotokan (Kanazawa ryu)
Distribution: Hertfordshire, Essex.
Mr P Perry
28 Folly Fields
Wheathampstead
Herts

Karatedo Shotokai
Style: Shotokai
Distribution: Birmingham,
Bedford, Tyne & Wear,
Manchester, Glos, Surrey
Mr A Baker
Redcliffe House
92c Whiteladies Road
Bristol
BS8 2QN
Tel: 0272 743535

Kateda School of Self Defence
Style: Kateda
Distribution: London & Essex
Mr P Davis
1 Chalford Court
Pershore Close
Barkingside, Essex

Katsu Karate Federation
Style: Wado ryu
Distribution: West Midlands
Mr E Cox
50 Cranmore Road
Newbridge
Wolverhampton
W Midlands

Kenyukai Karate Centres
Style: Shukokai based
Distribution: Manchester
North of England
Mrs L Stevens,
'Kusa Yama',
48, Clifton Drive,
Foxlow Park,
Buxton, Derby.
Tel: 0298 77362

Mr T Pottage
10, Thompson Road
Denton,
Manchester
M34 2PR
Tel: 061 336 2824

Kofu-Kan Shito-Ryu Do
Style: Shito ryu
Distribution: National
Mr T Murthwaite
119 Hallfields Lane
Gunthorpe
Peterborough
Tel: 0733 72399

Midlands Karate Federation
Style: Wado ryu
Distribution: West Midlands
Mr S Darkes,
14, Welford Road,
Sutton Coldfield
Warks.
Tel: 021 643 3731

Northern Karate Association
Style: Shotokan
Distribution: Yorks,
Humberside &
Newcastle-upon-Tyne
Miss W Murton
1 Denesway
Garforth
Leeds LS26 2AT

Phoenix Karate Organisation
Style: Wado ryu
Mr B Tatlow,
2 Moat Farm Drive
Bedworth
Warks
Tel: 0203 363959

Mr R Fowkes
15, Webster Road
Foleshill
Coventry CV6 5BB
Tel: 0203 664936

Sanchin Wado Kai
Style: Wado ryu
Distribution: West Midlands
Mr L Service
20 Haney Hay Road
The Triangle
Chasetown
Burntwood,
Walsall
West Midlands

Sei-Bu-Kan Wado-Kai Association
Style: Wado ryu + Kempo Karate
Distribution: Hampshire, Devon, Channel Islands
Mr W Evans
100 High Lawn Way
Havant
Hants

Seishinkai Shotokan Karate
Style: Shotokan
Distribution: Home Counties
Mr M Phipps
34 Crawley Drive
Hemel Hempstead
Herts HP2 6BS

Sentenashi Karate Kosai
Style: Anshinryu
Distribution: Co. Durham
Mr P Carbert
Sentenashi Karate Centre
107 Gladstone Street
Darlington

Shinji-Ryu Karate Association
Style: Shukokai
Distribution: Lancashire, Cheshire
Mr T Scott
5 Sunnybrow Road
Gorton
Manchester M18 7AE

Shorai Karate Association
Style: Shukokai
Distribution: Lancashire
Mr J F Tierney
8 Armstrong Street
Horwich
Lancashire, BL6 5PW

Shotokan Karate Association
Style: Shotokan
Distribution: North London, Middlesex, Herts
Mr M Randall
26 Poynter Road
Enfield
Middlesex

Shotokan Karate of Great Britain
Style: Shotokan
Distribution: Leicester & Nottingham
Mr J Edwards
31 Howard Close
Loughborough
Leicester

Shotokan Karate International
Style: Shotokan
Distribution: National
Mr A Hampson
185 Wollaton Road
Beeston
Nottingham

Shotoryu Karate Kai
Style: Shoto ryu
Distribution: North & South Devon & Channel Islands
Mr M Crooke
61 Haddington Road
Stoke, Plymouth
Devon

Shukokai Karate Federation
Style: Shukokai
Distribution: West Midlands,
Lancashire
Mr E Daniels
Shukokai Karate Centres
3–5 Park Street
Digbeth, Birmingham

Mr S Steward
55 Broadstone Road
Bradshaw
Bolton BL2 4AT

Sokudo Karate Association
Style: Shukokai
Distribution: N. England
Mr A Shaher
85 Acklam Road
Middlesborough
Cleveland

**South Of England Karate
Association**
Style: Wado ryu
Distribution: Surrey, Sussex
Hants
Mr P D Elliott,
54, Billingshurst Road
Broadbridge Heath
Nr. Horsham
Sussex

**South Of England Karate
Union**
Style: Shotokan
Distribution: South of England
Mr M V O'Donnell
25 East Street
Porchester
Nr. Fareham
Hants

Southern Karate-Do Wado-Kai
Style: Wado ryu
Distribution: South of
England
Mr B Wilkinson,
South View,
Folly Lane North,
Upper Hale,
Farnham,
Surrey GU9 0HU
Tel: 0252 723622

Sports Karate Organisation
Style: Free Style
Distribution: London
Mr D Mitchell
PO Box 159
London SE18 2NH

**Swanda-One Karate
Association**
Style: Swanda-One
Distribution: Cornwall
Macclesfield
Mr A Burgoyne
18 Hollins Road
Macclesfield
Cheshire

Takamizawa Institute of Karate
Style: Wado ryu
Distribution: National
Mr S Rowe,
159, Darnley Road,
Strood,
Rochester,
Kent ME2 2UH.
Tel: 0634 711372

Thames Karate – North
Style: Shotokan
Distribution: Merseyside &
Yorks
Mr R Colwell
2 Ribble Road
Gateacre
Liverpool 25

Thames Karate – South
Style: Shotokan
Distribution: London and
South East
Mr R Fuller
16 Netherwood Court
1 Lower Park Road
Belvedere
Kent

**Traditional Association of
Shotokan Karate**
Style: Shotokan
Distribution: Beds, North
Herts
Mr J van Weenan
Harlington Manor
Harlington
Bedfordshire

**Uechi Ryu Karate
Association G.B.**
Style: Uechi ryu
Distribution: Merseyside &
Home Counties
Dr D L Scott
21A Aigburth Drive
Liverpool L17 4JQ

Mr T Daly
19 Hermitage Road
Haringey
London N4 1DF

**United Kingdom Seiki-Jukyu
Karate Organisation**
Style: Seiki-Jukyu
Distribution: London
Mr F Perry
'Busen'
9 King Street
Twickenham
Surrey
Tel: 01-892-3338

United Kingdom Karate Jutsu
Style: Karate-Jutsu
Distribution: South of England
Mr B Dowler,
Walters Fladgate & Co
9 Queen Anne St
London W1M 0BQ
Tel: 01 637 5181

Unity Self Defence
Style: Self Defence
Distribution: London
Mr R McNeil
3 Colville Houses
London W11 1JB

Wessex Karate Association
Style: Wado ryu
Distribution: South of England
Mr M Simpson
11 Kingston Road
Poole
Dorset

Zenshin-Do Karate Association
Style: Shotokan
Distribution: Birmingham &
West Midlands
Mrs S Graham
10 Endicott Road
Aston
Birmingham

**For Clubs in Scotland, Wales or Northern Ireland
the following addresses will be useful**

**Scottish Karate Board of
Control**
Mr D Bryceland
74 Lamington Road
Glasgow G52 2SE
Scotland

Mr B Whelan
1 Berwick Place
Coatbridge
Scotland

Welsh Karate Federation
Mr K Mumberson
Smalldrink
Parsonage Lane
Begelly, Kilgetty
Dyfed

Northern Ireland Karate Board
Mr O Brunton
89 Brooke Drive
Belfast 11

Mr T Boyle
52 Raby Street
Ormeau Road
Belfast 2

Index